Structure & Speaking Practice
Cartagena

NATIONAL
GEOGRAPHIC
L E A R N I N G

Australia • Brazil • Mexico • Singapore • United Kingdom • United States

NATIONAL GEOGRAPHIC LEARNING

National Geographic Learning,
a Cengage Company

Structure & Speaking Practice, Cartagena

Nancy Douglas and James R. Morgan

Publisher: Sherrise Roehr

Executive Editor: Laura LeDréan

Managing Editor: Jennifer Monaghan

Digital Implementation Manager,
Irene Boixareu

Senior Media Researcher: Leila Hishmeh

Director of Global Marketing: Ian Martin

Regional Sales and National Account
Manager: Andrew O'Shea

Content Project Manager: Ruth Moore

Senior Designer: Lisa Trager

Manufacturing Planner: Mary Beth
Hennebury

Composition: Lumina Datamatics

For permission to use material from this text or product,
submit all requests online at **cengage.com/permissions**
Further permissions questions can be emailed to
permissionrequest@cengage.com

Student Edition: Structure & Speaking Practice, Cartagena
ISBN-13: 978-0-357-13792-5

National Geographic Learning
20 Channel Center Street
Boston, MA 02210
USA

Locate your local office at **international.cengage.com/region**

Visit National Geographic Learning online at **ELTNGL.com**
Visit our corporate website at **www.cengage.com**

Printed in China
Print Number: 02   Print Year: 2019

Photo Credits

SCOPE & SEQUENCE

	Unit / Lesson	Video	Vocabulary	Listening
UNIT 1 ALL ABOUT YOU p. 2				
	LESSON **A** Sports	Yoga in Schools	**Sports and activities** *swimming, tennis, surfing*	**From physician to beach bum** Use visual cues Make predictions Listen for gist and details
	LESSON **B** Personality		**Personality traits** *organized, messy, talkative, reserved*	**Personality types** Use visual cues Infer Listen for gist and details
UNIT 2 THE MIND p. 16				
	LESSON **A** Memory	The Sleep Test	**Can you remember?** *forget, good at remembering*	**There are things you can do.** Listen for main ideas Listen for details
	LESSON **B** Sleep		**Sleep** *stay up late, go to bed, get up*	**Sleep problems** Listen for gist Listen to sequence events
UNIT 3 CHANGE p. 30				
	LESSON **A** Habits	Keep Clean in 2015	**Life changes** *lose / find a job, be in good / bad shape*	**New Year's resolutions** Make predictions Listen for details
	LESSON **B** Goals		**After graduation** *goal, get ready, take it easy*	**A new singer** Listen for details Understand a speaker's attitude
UNIT 4 SHOPPING p. 44				
	LESSON **A** At the market	Field of Greens	**What foods are in your kitchen?** *chicken, fish, eggs*	**Shopping list** Use background knowledge Listen for gist Listen for details
	LESSON **B** Let's go shopping!		**Shopping** *credit card, on sale, a mall*	**Going to the store** Listen for gist Listen for details

Expansion Activities p. 58

Grammar	Pronunciation	Speaking	Reading	Writing	Communication
Verb + infinitive; verb + noun *How often...?* frequency expressions	Reduced *to*	Inviting and offering with *Do you want*	Life style Use background knowledge Make predictions Scan for information Read for details	Describe your personality	Guess a classmate's identity from survey answers Take a personality quiz and talk about the results
The simple past: affirmative and negative statements (irregular verbs) The simple past tense: question forms	Irregular past tense verbs	Expressing degrees of certainty	A study of sleep Identify the main idea Scan for details	Write about your sleep patterns	Recall and share childhood memories Ask and answer questions about sleep patterns
Like to / would like to The future with *be going to*	Contrastive stress	Making and responding to requests	A lifetime dream Make predictions Read for details Scan for information	Write about a future goal	Give advice about bad habits Talk about future goals
Count and noncount nouns Quantifiers with affirmative and negative statements	Syllables	Talking about things you need	On sale in Seoul Make predictions Identify main ideas Scan for details	Write about your favorite place to shop	Choose items to take on an island survival trip List items a person needs and say where to buy them

Language Summaries p. 66   Grammar Notes p. 69

1 ALL ABOUT YOU

Look at the photo. Answer the questions.

1 What are the people doing?

2 Can you do what they are doing?

3 What sports do you like to do?

UNIT GOALS

1 Talk about sports that you like and do

2 Invite and offer using *Do you want*

3 Describe different personalities

4 Talk about how often you do things

Photographers take photos of a surfer in Oahu, Hawaii, in the United States.

A group of children do yoga outside.

1 VIDEO Yoga in Schools

A 🔄 Look at the picture. Have you seen people do this before? Does it look fun? Tell a partner.

B ▶ You are going to watch a video about teaching yoga in school. Read the sentences. What do people say about yoga? Fill in the missing words.

1. "Sometimes it takes a lot of courage to just be a little bit more still and not _____."
2. "I forget about the _____ things that are happening."
3. "I feel _____ and calm."
4. "Before, I'm always just running around and not really paying attention, but after yoga, I feel, like _____ and can do my work faster."
5. "Yoga is simply a _____..."
6. "_____% of our students say that after yoga class, they are more ready to learn."

C 🔄 Look at your answers in **B**. Did the students enjoy their yoga class? Explain your answer to a partner.

D 🔄 Is having a yoga class in your school a good idea? Why or why not? Tell your partner.

2 VOCABULARY

A 🔷 The sports words in each column are missing the same vowel (*a, e, i, o,* or *u*). Fill in the missing letters. Work with a partner. Which words go with *play* or *do*? with *go*?

1. b___seb___ll

2. b___sketb___ll

3. volleyb___ll

4. b___dminton

5. sw___mm___ng

6. p___ng pong

7. surf___ng

8. sk___ ___ng

9. y___ga

10. jud___

11. b___wling

12. j___gging

13. hock___y

14. t___nnis

15. socc___r

16. pilat___s

B 🔷 Ask a partner these questions.

1. Can you play _____ well?

2. Name one person who does _____. Why are they good at it?

3. When was the last time you went _____? How was it?

> Can you play volleyball well?

> No, I can't. I'm too short!

ℹ️ **play / do** + noun
You **play** a <u>game</u> of *soccer, basketball,* etc.
Also with **play**: *cards, darts, golf, rugby*
You **do** martial arts (*judo, kickboxing,* etc.) and other activities. Also with **do**: *gymnastics, crafts, puzzles*

go + noun + *-ing*
You can often do activities with **go** alone. Also with **go**: *camping, climbing, fishing, golfing*

3 LISTENING

A **Use visual cues.** Look at the title in **B** and the photo at the bottom of the page. What is this listening about?

B 🔊 🗣 **Make predictions.** Read the paragraph. Then listen and complete it. Answer the question below. **Track 1**

From Physician to Beach Bum

In the 1950s, Dorian "Doc" Paskowitz was a successful physician. He was handsome and in good health. To many people, Doc's life seemed perfect. But it wasn't. Doc was _____. He didn't like his work. The one thing he loved was _____. So one day, Doc decided to change his life. He decided to follow his _____.

What do you think happened to Doc Paskowitz and his family? Circle your answer(s). Then explain your ideas to a partner.

a. He surfed all the time.   c. He traveled with his family.

b. He became a doctor in another city.   d. He built a house on the beach.

C 🔊 **Listen for gist.** Listen to more of the story and complete the sentences. **Track 2**

1. Doc and his wife had _____.   2. The family became a _____.

D 🔊 **Listen for details.** Listen to the rest of the story and choose the correct answer for each item. **Track 3**

1. They lived _____.
   a. in a small camper   b. a busy life
2. They visited places like _____.
   a. California and Australia   b. Mexico and Venezuela
3. The family had _____.
   a. a lot of money   b. a small business
4. The children did not _____.
   a. go to school   b. learn to surf well

E 🗣 What do you think of the Paskowitz family? Did they have a good life? Why or why not? Discuss with a partner.

4 SPEAKING

A 🔊 Listen to the conversation. Underline Connie's offer. Circle Gina's invitation. **Track 4**

CONNIE: Hey, Gina. Do you want some ice cream?

GINA: No, thanks. I'm going out.

CONNIE: Really? Where are you going?

GINA: I'm going to play tennis. Do you want to come?

CONNIE: Sorry, I can't. I need to study.

GINA: Well, come later then. We're playing all afternoon.

CONNIE: It sounds nice... but I'm not very good at tennis.

GINA: Don't worry about that. You don't have to play. You can just watch. Come on, it'll be fun.

CONNIE: Well, OK. I'll see you in an hour.

GINA: OK, see you later... and maybe we can have some ice cream afterwards!

B 🔄 Practice the conversation with a partner.

SPEAKING STRATEGY

C Complete the information below.

1. Sport or activity I like to do: _____

2. Place to do it: _____

3. Day / time to do it: _____

D 🔄 Make a conversation with a partner. Use the conversation above and the Useful Expressions to help you. Follow the steps below.

1. Invite your partner to do your activity.

2. Your partner should first decline the invitation.

3. Next, your partner accepts it.

4. Switch roles and repeat.

E 🔄 Perform one of your conversations for the class.

Useful Expressions	
Inviting and offering with *Do you want*	
Inviting	Do you want to come? [*want* + *to* + verb] Sure, I'd love to! Sorry, I can't. I'm busy. Um, no thanks. I'm not good at...
Offering	Do you want some ice cream? [*want* + noun] Yes, please. / Yes, thanks. No, thank you. / No, thanks. I'm fine.
Speaking tip	
You can also use *would like* to invite: *Would you like to come with us?*	

5 GRAMMAR

A Turn to page 69. Complete the exercise. Then do **B–D** below.

Verb + Infinitive	Verb + Noun
I **love** / **like** <u>to play</u> volleyball.	I **love** / **like** <u>sports</u>.
I **forgot** <u>to explain</u> the rules.	I **need** my <u>uniform</u>.

Verbs like *forget, hate, learn, like, love, need, decide, plan, prepare,* and *want* can be followed by a noun or the infinitive (*to* + the base form of the verb).

B 🔊 **Pronunciation: Reduced *to*.** Listen and repeat. What do you notice about the pronunciation of the word *to* in each sentence? **Track 5**

1. I like to play golf.
2. She likes to go jogging.
3. I love to sleep late.
4. He hates to study.

5. We plan to fly to Paris.
6. Do you like to play chess?
7. I want to be early.
8. I hate to be late.

C This is Jenna. For each picture, make up a sentence about her or the people she's with. Use the verbs given.

D 🔄 Ask and answer the questions with a partner.

What is one thing…

    you love to do on the weekend?

    you need to study harder?

    you want to do by the end of the year?

What are two things…

    you plan to do soon?

    you want for your next birthday?

    you like about your school?

> What are two things you like about your school?

> Let's see… I like my classmates. They're friendly. And I also like…

6 COMMUNICATION

A   Read the questions below. Write your answers under *My answer* in the chart.

	My answer	Classmate's name	Classmate's answer
1. What's your favorite sport or event to watch?			
2. Which sport do you most like to play?			
3. Who's your favorite athlete?			
4. What do you want for your birthday?			
5. What movie do you want to see?			
6. What is one thing you learned in the last year?			
7. Where do you plan to go next year?			
8. What do you want to do this weekend?			

B   For each question, interview a *different* classmate. Write each person's name and answer in the chart.

C   Get into a group of three. For each question, read a classmate's answer. Do *not* say the person's name. Your group guesses which classmate gave that answer.

I asked the question, "What's your favorite sport or event to watch?" This person loves to watch soccer.

I know! That's Mateo.

Yes, that's right!

Penny and Pearl are both friendly. They are also **bright** (intelligent). However, their friends say they are very different.

Penny

Pearl

Penny is very **organized**. She knows where everything is in her apartment.

Penny is really **ambitious**. Someday, she wants to have her own company.

Penny's very **careful** with her money. In fact, she's a little bit **selfish**—sometimes she doesn't like to share.

Penny is somewhat **reserved**. She has two or three close friends and doesn't go out a lot.

Pearl's apartment is kind of **messy**: there are dirty dishes in the sink and magazines on the floor.

Pearl is very **laid-back** (relaxed) about life and work.

Sometimes Pearl is **careless** with money—she forgets to pay her bills.

But she's very **generous**. She will share anything with you.

Pearl is **talkative**. She talks to everyone and is comfortable at parties.

1 VOCABULARY

> **i** You can use these words to make adjectives stronger:
> **very** organized   **really** ambitious
> You can use these words to weaken negative adjectives:
> **a little (bit)** selfish   **somewhat** reserved   **kind of** messy

A 🔁 Penny and Pearl are cousins. Read about their personalities. Then answer the questions with a partner.

1. Which words in **blue** are opposites?

2. Which words do you think are positive? Which are negative?

B Look at the pictures. Which items belong to Pearl? to Penny? How do you know? Write their names.

1. _____   2. _____   3. _____   4. _____

C 🗨 Which words in blue do you think describe Penny? Which describe Pearl? Explain your answers to a partner.

A **competitive** person wants to be more successful than other people.

An **impulsive** person does things suddenly without thinking carefully.

A **creative** person has a lot of new ideas, especially in the arts (music, dance, etc.).

A **private** person doesn't like others to know how he or she feels.

D 🗨 Is your personality more like Pearl's or Penny's? How? Tell a partner.

2 LISTENING

A **Use visual cues.** Look at the photos. What are the people doing? Guess: How do the people feel?

Word Bank
Opposites
patient ↔ impatient

B 🔊 **Infer; Listen for gist.** A man is going to talk about two personality types: Type A and Type B. Listen and circle the correct answer. **Track 6**

1. The talk is happening at a company / hospital / school.

2. Photo 1 / Photo 2 / Both photos above show(s) a Type A person.

C 🔊 **Listen for details.** Look up any unfamiliar words below. Then listen again. Which words describe a Type A person? Check (✓) them. **Track 6**

☐ angry   ☐ laid-back   ☐ patient

☐ competitive ☐ nervous   ☐ a workaholic

D 🗨 Answer the questions with a partner.

1. Guess: What words describe a Type B person? Make a list of your ideas.

2. Are you more Type A or Type B? Why?

3. "Being Type A can be bad for your health." Do you agree or disagree with this sentence? Why?

A **Use background knowledge.** Look at the title of the reading and the four personality types. Do you know about any of the people in the photos? What do they do?

B **Make predictions.** Guess the answers about the four personality types. Sometimes more than one answer is possible.

This person...	The Dreamer	The Partner	The Thinker	The Artist
1. likes to follow rules.		✓		
2. is creative.				
3. listens to others' opinions.				
4. is a problem solver.				
5. has strong ideas about things.				
6. is careful.				
7. is organized and helpful.				
8. doesn't like change.				
9. does things without thinking carefully.				

C **Scan for information.** Look quickly at the reading to find the answers in **B**. Correct any incorrect answers.

D 🔗 **Read for details.** Read the passage again. Which one or two of the personality types describe(s) you? your best friend? your parents? Why? Tell a partner.

> I'm a mix of the Dreamer and the Artist.

LIFE STYLE

Malala Yousafzai

The Dreamer

A Dreamer thinks there is a "right" way to do things. This person wants to live in the "perfect world." A Dreamer is often hardworking, organized, and very passionate[1] about his or her work. Many are good listeners and want to help others. Many Dreamers work as activists, lawyers, and in leadership roles.

[1]If you are *passionate* about something, you care about it a lot.

The Partner

A Partner wants to be in a group. For this person, rules and group harmony are important. Tradition is, too. Partners are often reserved, careful people, and change makes them nervous. Many do well as managers, police officers, and politicians.

Famous Partners: Queen Elizabeth II, UN Secretary-General Ban Ki-Moon

Ban Ki-Moon

The Thinker

For Thinkers, understanding things is very important. They like to solve problems and make new things. Thinkers can also be competitive. They like to win. They are careful, ambitious people and often have very strong opinions. Many Thinkers work as scientists, inventors, politicians, and engineers.

Famous Thinkers: filmmaker and inventor James Cameron, scientist Stephen Hawking, businesswoman Sheryl Sandberg

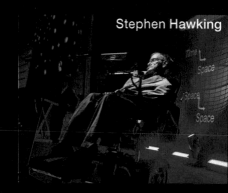
Stephen Hawking

The Artist

Artists want to be free. They don't want to follow the rules all the time. Artists like action and are often impulsive. They also like trying new things, and they aren't afraid of change. Like Thinkers, many Artists have strong opinions. They do well in creative fields like music, acting, design, and in some sports.

Famous Artists: fashion designer Yang Li, soccer player Luis Suárez, singer Beyoncé

Beyoncé

Famous Dreamers: activist Malala Yousafzai, lawyer Amal Ramzi Clooney, journalist and food activist Carlo Petrini

4 GRAMMAR

A Turn to pages 69–70. Complete the exercises. Then do **B** and **C** below.

How often...? Frequency Expressions			
How often do you see your best friend?	(I see her)	**every**	day / Monday / week / month / summer.
		once **twice** **three times** **several times**	a day / a week / a month / a year.
		all the time. **once in a while.**	
	Hardly ever.		

B Answer the questions about yourself.

How often do you...   Answer

1. go shopping and spend too much money?   I spend too much money once in a while _____.

2. watch TV?   _____.

3. buy things for your friends or family?   _____.

4. play video games and win?   _____.

5. go on dates?   _____.

6. text your friends?   _____.

7. clean your desk?   _____.

8. stay up late studying or working?   _____.

C 🔄 Take turns asking and answering the questions in **B** with a partner.
Are you similar or different?

> I play games and win all the time. I'm really competitive.

> I only clean my desk once in a while. I'm kind of messy.

5 WRITING

A Read the student's personality profile. What adjectives does he use to describe himself? Circle them.

> ## What are you like?
>
> Usually, I'm kind of shy. For example, I like to go to parties, but it's hard to talk to new people. I feel nervous, so I'm kind of quiet. But once you get to know me, I'm really talkative. I like to tell jokes, and I'm very funny. I'm also a little competitive. I play video games with my friends all the time, and I hate to lose. For this reason, they hardly ever win!

B Think of three personality adjectives to describe yourself. Write them below. Also use one of the words given with the adjective.

I'm very / kind of / a little _____.

I'm very / kind of / a little _____.

I'm very / kind of / a little _____.

C Write about yourself. Remember to explain each idea in **B** with an example.

D 🔾 Exchange your paper with a partner. Circle any mistakes. Then answer the question in **A** about your partner. Did you learn anything new about him or her? Tell the class.

6 COMMUNICATION

A 🔾 Use the chart to interview a partner. Circle his or her answers.

Personality Quiz

Questions	Answers	
How often do you clean your room?	**a.** once a week	**b.** once in a while
How often do friends ask for your advice?	**a.** all the time	**b.** hardly ever
What is more important?	**a.** being kind	**b.** being honest
What is more important?	**a.** agreeing with the group	**b.** saying my opinion
Are you careful with money?	**a.** Yes, most of the time.	**b.** No, not really.
What is more important to you?	**a.** success	**b.** happiness
You're playing a game. Which sentence describes you?	**a.** I'm very competitive. I hate to lose.	**b.** I'm kind of laid-back. I want to win, but if I lose, it's OK.
Your cell phone isn't working. What do you do?	**a.** try to fix it myself	**b.** ask for help
What is more important?	**a.** facts	**b.** feelings
What do you want in your life?	**a.** many different experiences	**b.** the same job
What is more important?	**a.** being free	**b.** being careful
You get a free ticket to Paris. The plane leaves tomorrow. Do you go?	**a.** Yes! I'm very impulsive.	**b.** No way! That's too scary.

B 🔾 Total your partner's points for each color (a = 2 points, b = 1 point). Read about the color(s) with the *most* points on page 85 and tell your partner about his or her personality type(s).

C 🔾 Do you agree with your description? Explain your opinion to your partner.

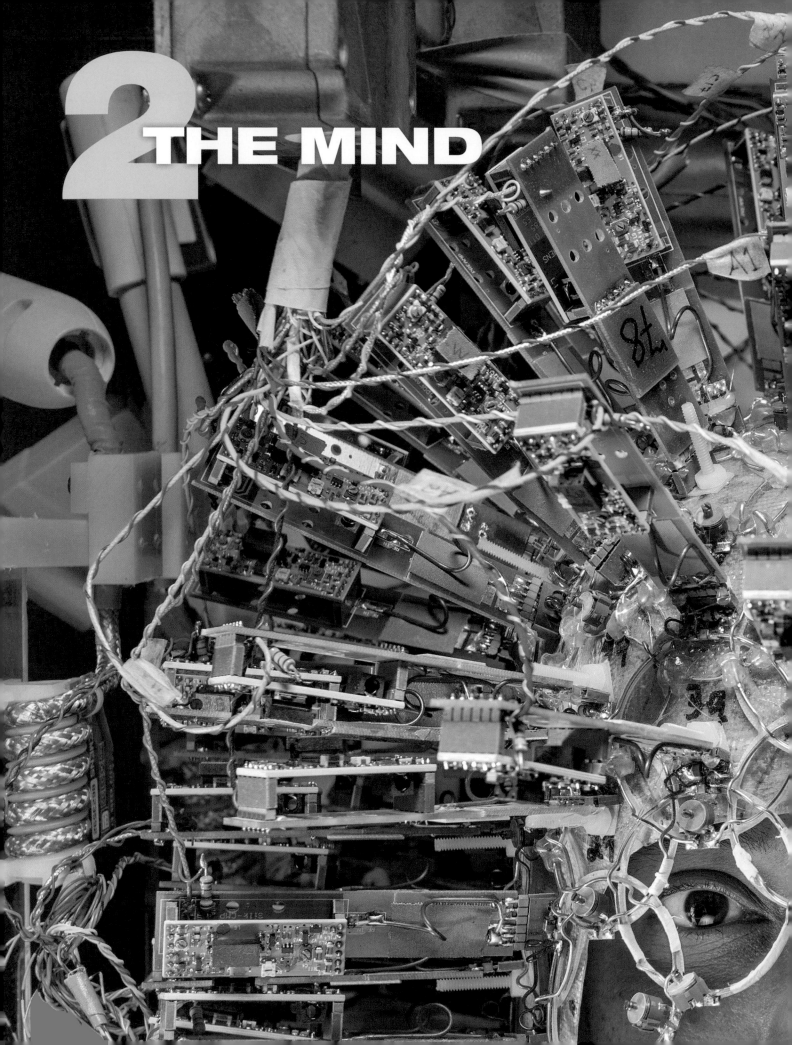

2 THE MIND

Look at the photo. Answer the questions.

1 Where is the man?

2 What is the machine doing?

3 What can doctors learn from this research?

UNIT GOALS

1 Talk about important memories

2 Express degrees of certainty

3 Talk about your sleep habits

4 Ask and answer questions about a past experience

A machine studies a man's brain at a
Harvard University research hospital.

A man falls asleep on a city bus.

1 VIDEO The Sleep Test

A 🔄 Look at the Word Bank. Then ask a partner: Are you sleep deprived?

B ▶ Watch the first 30 seconds of the video with the sound off. Circle the changes you see. Then watch with the sound on to check your answers.

the buildings disappear   the clouds get bigger

the bus changes color   the child runs toward the road

C ▶ Read the questions and review the meaning of the words in **bold** with your instructor. Then watch the whole video and write a word to complete each question.

1. Do you need an alarm _____ to **wake up**?

2. Do you **fall asleep** after _____ minutes in bed?

3. Do you drink a lot of _____ or energy drinks to **stay awake**?

D 🔄 Ask and answer the questions in **C** with a partner.

2 VOCABULARY

"Hi, I think I know you..."

A 🔄 Read the sentences in the chart about memory. How many of them are true for you? Compare your answers with a partner's.

Word Bank
Opposites
remember ←————→ forget
(to keep information in your mind) (to not remember)

	Yes	No
1. I sometimes **forget** to do my homework.	☐	☐
2. When I leave the house, I never **forget** my house key.	☐	☐
3. I'm **good at remembering** people's names.	☐	☐
4. I **can** always **remember** my friends' birthdays.	☐	☐
5. I **have** an excellent **memory**.	☐	☐
6. Looking at old photos **brings back** many happy **memories**.	☐	☐
7. I **can** sing a song in English **from memory**.	☐	☐
8. **I'll never forget the day** I graduated from school.	☐	☐

B 🔄 Complete these sentences with your own ideas. Discuss your answers with a partner.

1. I sometimes forget to _____.
2. When I leave the house, I never forget my _____.
3. I'm good at remembering _____.
4. I always remember _____ birthday(s).
5. I have a(n) _____ memory.
6. _____ brings back many happy memories.
7. I can _____ from memory.
8. I'll never forget the day I _____.

Word Bank
Words used to talk about memory
have a(n) excellent / sharp / good / bad / poor memory
a happy / good / sad / painful memory

During the day, I sometimes forget to check my email.

Not me! I check mine every 10 minutes!

3 LISTENING

A Are you good at remembering new words in English? Why or why not? Tell a partner.

B 🔊 **Listen for main ideas.** Listen to part of Galina and Tomo's conversation. Circle the correct answer to complete each sentence. **Track 8**

1. They're talking about a _____ .

   a. word   b. test   c. dictionary

2. Tomo is worried because _____ .

   a. he thinks he did poorly   b. he just got a bad grade   c. he has a lot of homework

C 🔊 **Listen for details.** Listen to the entire conversation. Look at the pictures. Check (✓) the things Galina does. **Track 9**

D Read these methods for learning new vocabulary in English. Which ones do you like? Discuss with a partner. How do you remember new words in English?

- Practice saying the new word again and again.

- Put important new words in places where you will see them during the day (on your laptop or on the bathroom mirror, for example). Every time you see the word, say it aloud.

- Exchange new information with the word. For example, for *beach*, ask a friend, *What's your favorite beach?*

- Make a sentence using the word. Use real people and facts from your life in the sentence.

- Listen to a story in English. At the same time, read the story in your own language.

- Your idea: _____ .

If you travel to a country where people speak English, practice speaking with the people there.

4 SPEAKING

A 🔊 Listen to Mia and Justin's conversation. Where do you think they're going? What is Justin looking for? **Track 10**

MIA: I'm so excited! Are you ready to go in?

JUSTIN: Um... just a minute. I can't find the tickets.

MIA: You're kidding!

JUSTIN: No, I'm not. I put them in my front pocket. See? They're not there.

MIA: Well, are they in your backpack?

JUSTIN: I don't think so.

MIA: Maybe you dropped them somewhere.

JUSTIN: Maybe. I'm not sure.

MIA: Oh, Justin. What are we going to do?

JUSTIN: Wait... hold on. I found them. They were in my *back* pocket.

MIA: Great! Let's go!

B 🔁 Practice the conversation with a partner.

SPEAKING STRATEGY

C 🔁 Read the questions below. Add your own question for each topic. Then take turns asking and answering the questions with a partner. Use the Useful Expressions in your answers.

Your instructor	Your partner
Is your instructor married? Does your instructor like vegetables? Your question: _____	Does your partner live near you? Does your partner like rap music? Your question: _____
Your school	**Public schools in the US**
Are there a lot of restaurants near your school? Is there a bus stop near your school? Your question: _____	Do students wear uniforms? Does the school year start in the fall? Your question: _____

Useful Expressions
Expressing degrees of certainty
Are they in your backpack?
Yes, they are. / No, they aren't. (very certain)
I think so. / I don't think so. (less certain)
Maybe. I'm not sure. (not very certain)
I have no idea. (= I don't know.)

5 GRAMMAR See pages 79–81 for review on regular forms of the simple past.

A Turn to page 71. Complete the exercises. Then do **B–D** below.

The Simple Past: Affirmative and Negative Statements (Irregular Verbs)			
Subject	***did + not***	**Verb**	
I / You / He / She / We / They		forgot	her birthday.
	didn't	forget	

B 🔊 **Pronunciation: Irregular past tense verbs.** Practice saying the verb pairs in row A aloud. Then listen and repeat. Can you guess the pronunciation for the verbs in row B? Say them aloud. Then listen and repeat. **Track 11**

Row A	forget / forgot	tell / told	ring / rang	keep / kept	understand / understood
Row B	get / got	sell / sold	sing / sang	sleep / slept	stand / stood

C 🔁 Work with a partner. Follow the steps below to create sentences in a story.

1. Start at ❶.
2. Using only horizontal and vertical lines, connect the words to form a sentence. The words with punctuation end a sentence.
3. Write the sentence in the blanks below, changing the verbs from the present to the past tense.
4. Repeat with ❷, ❸, and so on.
5. Read the story aloud with your partner.

❶		❺ He	says	Hi	Teddy	how	are
go	to	comes	over	to	me.	you?
❷ At	a	and	smiles	❹ He	don't	❻ I
the	party	at	his	name.	know	what
party	friend's	my	remember	don't	say.	to
I	house.	from	my	❸ I	❼ I	embarrassed!
see	a	student	old	school.	am	so

❶ __I__ __went__ __to__ __a__ __party__ __at__ __my__ __friend's__ __house__.

❷ __At__ __the__ __party__, _____ _____ _____ _____ _____ _____ _____ _____

❸ _____ _____ _____ _____ _____ _____ _____

❹ _____ _____ _____ _____ _____ _____

❺ _____ _____, " _____ , _____ , _____ _____ _____ "

❻ _____ _____ _____ _____

❼ _____ _____ _____ _____

D  Use one of these ideas, or your own ideas, to tell a story. What did you do?

Tell a partner when you...

- left something important at home.
- forgot someone's name.
- couldn't remember an answer on a test.

6 COMMUNICATION

A What are some of your childhood memories? They can be happy, good, sad, or other memories. Make notes about your ideas in the chart.

A memory about...	Notes
my house or apartment.	
my parents.	
my brother(s) or sister(s).	
my grandparents.	
a favorite food.	
a friend.	
a toy.	
music.	
school.	
a vacation.	

B Get together with a partner. Take turns telling each other your memories.

> I have a happy memory about my old apartment. We lived on the second floor. Every day, I played with my best friend Lin.

C Discuss the questions with your partner.

1. Are any of your memories similar to your partner's?
2. Which memory is your favorite?

D Share your partner's favorite memory with the class.

Sleep helps you think and remember information better, studies show.
A 20-minute nap during the day can also improve your mood and memory.

1 VOCABULARY

A Review the meaning of the words in **blue** with your instructor.
Then circle a or b to complete the sentences about yourself.

Word Bank
Opposites
(be) asleep ↔ (be) awake
fall asleep ↔ wake up
go to bed ↔ stay up (late)
get up ↔ stay in bed

1. I usually _____ every night.
   a. **go to bed** at 10:00 or 11:00   b. **stay up late** (midnight or later)

2. In bed, I _____.
   a. **fall asleep** quickly   b. **am awake** for a long time

3. I _____ **wake up** at night.
   a. hardly ever   b. often

4. In the morning, I usually _____.
   a. **get up** (from bed) right away   b. **stay in bed** for a while

B 🗣 Tell a partner your answers in **A**. Your partner asks you one follow-up question.

> I usually stay up late every night.

> Really? When do you go to bed?

> At midnight.

C 👥 Are you and your partner similar or different? How? Tell another pair.

2 LISTENING

A  Look at the three sleep problems below. Do you know anyone with these problems? Tell a partner.

Some people...

- can't sleep.
- have *nightmares* (bad dreams).
- are *sleepwalkers*. (They wake up at night and do things, but they are asleep.)

> Sometimes my brother has nightmares.

B 🔊 **Listen for gist.** Listen to a news program about a woman named Mary. What is her problem? **Track 12**

Mary _____.

a. has nightmares

b. is a sleepwalker

c. can't sleep

C 🔊  **Listen to sequence events.** Listen again. Put the events in order from 1 to 6. Then tell a partner Mary's story in your own words. **Track 12**

_____ Mary went to bed at 10:00.

_____ She tried to buy ice cream.

_____ The police drove Mary home.

_____ She drove away.

_____ She got up later that night.

_____ The police woke her up.

Word Bank	
Present	**Past**
drive	drove
wake up	woke up

D  What caused Mary's problem? Choose a possible answer. Explain it to a partner.

Maybe Mary...

- was worried about something.
- was hungry.
- had a nightmare.
- my idea: _____.

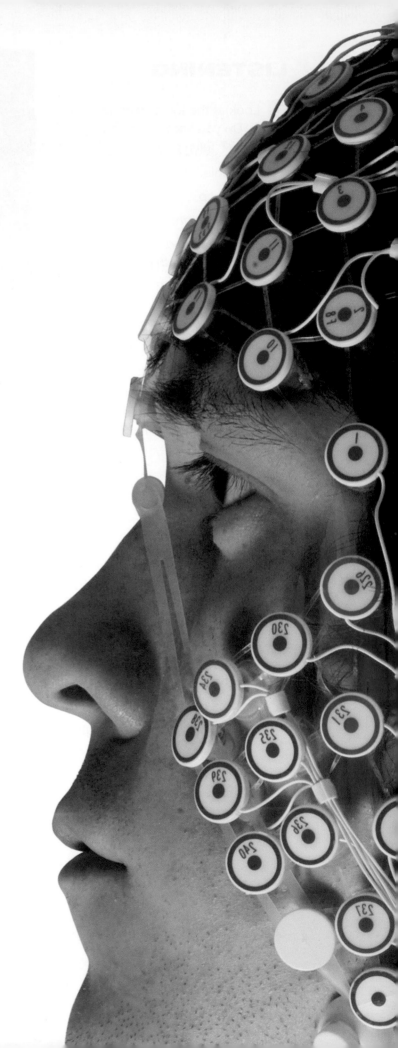

3 READING 🔊 Track 13

A 👥 Discuss the questions in a small group. Then compare your answers with the class.

1. How many hours do you sleep each night?

2. What do you do when you can't sleep?

B **Identify the main idea.** Read the article. Then circle the correct answer to the question.

What is the main point of the article?

a. Today, people have healthier sleep patterns.

b. Waking up at night is not good for you.

c. It's normal to wake up at night.

d. Sleep research has a lot of problems.

C **Scan for details.** Read quickly to find answers to complete the chart.

Sleep Patterns	
People are in bed but are awake.	2 hours
People sleep.	
	1–3 hours
	4–5 hours

D 🔄 Answer the questions with a partner.

1. What do you think of the sleep pattern described in the article? Is it healthy? Why or why not?

2. What would Dr. Wehr say: Are your sleep patterns healthy? Why or why not?

A STUDY OF SLEEP

A man wears special sensors in a sleep study.

It's 3:30 in the morning. Tomorrow is a busy day. You went to bed at 10:00. You need to get up at 6:00 in the morning. But you woke up in the middle of the night[1] and you can't fall asleep again! Why can't you sleep?

There may be a surprising answer. Dr. Thomas Wehr did some research on sleep. During the winter, he put people in a room with no artificial light (there was no light from lamps, TVs, or computers). Then, during the night, he studied the people's sleep patterns.[2]

What happened? The people went to bed, but they didn't fall asleep right away. Most were awake for two hours. Next, the people slept for four to five hours. Then they woke up, and they stayed awake and were active for one to three hours. Finally, the people slept again for four to five hours.

Dr. Wehr discovered a new sleep pattern. But maybe it's not new. In the past, before electric light, perhaps people slept this way. Nowadays, we sleep in a different way.

So, the next time you wake up in the middle of the night and can't sleep, relax! Your sleep patterns may be normal after all.

[1]If something happens *in the middle of the night*, it happens late at night, usually between 2:00 and 4:00 AM.

[2]A *pattern* is a repeated or regular way something happens.

4 GRAMMAR

A Turn to page 72. Complete the exercises. Then do **B–D** below.

The Simple Past Tense: *Yes / No* Questions				
Did	**Subject**	**Verb**		**Short Answers**
Did	you he they	stay up late wake up	last night?	Yes, I did. / No, I didn't. Yes, he did. / No, he didn't. Yes, they did. / No, they didn't.

The Simple Past Tense: *Wh-* Questions				
Wh- word	**did**	**Subject**	**Verb**	**Answers**
When	did	you she they	study?	(I / She / They studied) last night.
			get up?	(I / She / They got up) at 7:00.
What			happened to you?	I woke up late this morning.

B Complete the conversation with past tense questions and answers using the words in parentheses. Then practice the conversation with a partner.

A: (1. you / go out) _Did you go out_ last night?

B: No, (2.) _____. I (3. stay) _____ home and (4. watch) _____ a movie.

A: Really? (5. what / you / watch) _____?

B: An old zombie movie called *28 Days Later*.

A: (6. you / like) _____ it?

B: Yes, (7.) _____, but later I (8. have) _____ nightmares.

A: (9. why / you / have) _____ nightmares?

B: Because it was a very scary movie! (10. what / you / do) _____ last night?

A: I (11. go) _____ to a party.

B: (12. who / you / go) _____ with?

A: Margo.

B: (13. you / have) _____ fun?

A: Yeah, we (14. have) _____ a great time at first. But then, something strange happened.

C What strange thing happened to speaker A? Continue the conversation with your partner. Ask and answer four more past-tense questions to finish the story.

D Role-play your conversation for another pair. Whose story is the best?

5 WRITING

A Complete the paragraph with time words from the box.

finally	next	last	then	until

B 🗣 Read the paragraph and answer the questions with a partner.

1. When was the last time the writer stayed up late?
2. What did he do?
3. What time did he get up the next day?

C Answer the questions in **B** so they are true for you. Then use your notes and the words in **A** to write your own paragraph.

D 🗣 Exchange your writing with a partner. Read his or her paragraph.

1. Are there any mistakes? If yes, circle them.
2. Answer the questions in **B** about your partner's writing.

> _____ Saturday, I stayed up late. I watched TV _____ 10:00, and ___*then*___ I played video games _____ 12:30. I went to bed at 1:00, but I couldn't fall asleep! To relax, I listened to music and _____, I fell asleep at 3:00 AM. The _____ morning, I didn't get up _____ 11:00. I felt great, but my dad wasn't happy. He says I'm lazy!

6 COMMUNICATION

A Think about your sleep patterns for the last three days. Complete the chart.

	Yesterday	The Day Before Yesterday	Three Days Ago
Time I got up			
Time I went to bed			

B Use the words to write past tense *Yes / No* or *Wh-* questions.

1. what time / you / get up?
2. what time / you / go to bed?
3. you / fall asleep / right away?
4. you / wake up / during the night?
5. how many / hours / you / sleep?
6. what / you / dream / about?

> What time did you go to bed yesterday?
>
> I went to bed at 11.

C 🗣 Ask a partner the questions in **B** about the last three days. Take notes.

D 🗣 Read the sleep facts. Then answer the questions with a partner.

- Adults need seven to eight hours of sleep a night.
- It's best to go to bed and wake up at the same time each day.
- Light from computers and cell phones keeps you awake.

1. Do you and your partner have good sleep habits? Why or why not? Use your answers in **C** to explain.
2. What are two things you can do to sleep better?

E Share your answers in **D** with the class.

3 CHANGE

People do yoga at the Red Rocks
Amphitheatre, Colorado, US.

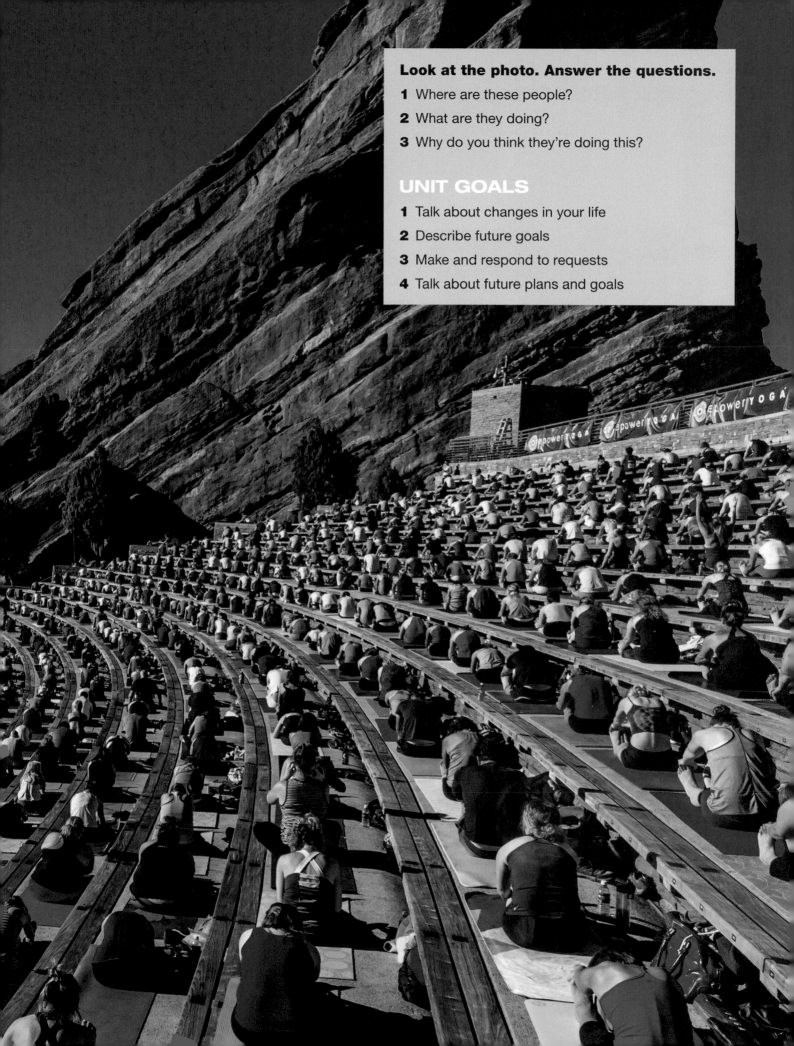

Look at the photo. Answer the questions.

1 Where are these people?

2 What are they doing?

3 Why do you think they're doing this?

UNIT GOALS

1 Talk about changes in your life

2 Describe future goals

3 Make and respond to requests

4 Talk about future plans and goals

1 **VIDEO** Keep Clean in 2015

A 🔄 Do you do any chores? Which ones? Can you think of ways to make them easier to do? Tell a partner.

B ▶ Watch the video. Put the advice in the correct order.

_____ Make a schedule.

_____ Always make progress.

_____ Set realistic goals.

_____ Stay focused.

_____ Reward yourself.

C 🔄 Can you think of any other advice for making changes like this? Tell a partner.

2 VOCABULARY

A Look at the two pictures of Martin. How are they different? Tell your partner one or two differences.

> In the first picture, Martin is working at home. In the second...

last year

this year

B Look at the picture of Martin this year. His life has changed a lot. Which sentences describe his changes? Circle the correct sentence.

1. Martin **lost his job**. / Martin **found a new job**.

2. He's **making** more **money**. / He's **making** less **money**.

3. He **lost weight**. / He **gained weight**.

4. He exercises a lot now. He's **in good shape**. / He's **in bad shape**.

5. He **started** smok**ing**. / He **stopped** smok**ing**.

Word Bank
found a new job = **got a new job**
making more money = **earning more money**
in bad shape = **out of shape**
stopped smoking = **quit smoking**

ℹ️ The words *stop*, *quit*, and *start* are often followed by a word ending in *-ing*:
He **stopped** <u>smoking</u> and **started** <u>exercising</u>.
Please **quit** <u>talking</u> and **start** <u>working</u>.

C What do you want to do this year? Circle your answer(s). Tell a partner.

get in shape   earn more money

find a new job   start / quit _____

other idea: _____

3 LISTENING

A 🔊 **Pronunciation: Contrastive stress.** Read the sentences. Then listen and repeat. **Track 14**

1. She <u>got</u> a new job. She's really happy about it.

2. You're in really <u>good</u> shape! How often do you work out?

3. He <u>stopped</u> smoking. That's great!

B 🔊 🔁 **Pronunciation: Contrastive stress.** Now listen to three dialogs. Underline the new information that is stressed in each response. Then practice the dialogs with a partner. **Track 15**

Many cultures celebrate the New Year as a time to start over. The celebration in Brazil includes fireworks.

   A: Is she making more money in her new job?
   B: No, she's making less money.

   A: How's your diet going? Did you lose weight or gain weight?
   B: Unfortunately, I gained two kilos.

   A: I heard that you quit drinking soda recently.
   B: No, actually, I quit drinking coffee.

C 🔁 Many people make changes, or resolutions, at the New Year. What is one change you tried to make in the past? Tell a partner.

D 🔊 **Make predictions.** Before you listen, read the sentences. Guess the answers. Then listen and complete the definition. **Track 16**

A New Year's resolution is a kind of personal _____ you make. You decide to make a _____ in the New Year and work very _____ to do it.

E 🔊 🔁 **Listen for details.** What are Jamal and Lea's resolutions? Write *J* for Jamal and *L* for Lea. (There are two extra.) Do you share any resolutions with Jamal or Lea? If so which one(s)? Tell a partner. **Track 17**

_____ 1. get better grades

_____ 2. find a part-time job

_____ 3. join a gym

_____ 4. earn money

_____ 5. lose weight

_____ 6. gain weight

4 SPEAKING

A 🔊 Listen to the conversation. What does Zack want from Juan? How does he ask for it? **Track 18**

ZACK: See you later, Juan. I'm going out for a while.

JUAN: OK, see you.

ZACK: Oh no!

JUAN: What?

ZACK: I forgot to go to the ATM.

JUAN: Do you need money?

ZACK: Yeah, I'd like to get a haircut this afternoon. Can I borrow $20?

JUAN: Sure, here you go.

ZACK: Thanks a lot.

B 👥 Practice the conversation with a partner.

SPEAKING STRATEGY

C 👥 Choose an item from the box. Ask to borrow it from your partner and give a reason. Use the Useful Expressions to help you create a conversation.

your partner's phone

some money

your partner's car

your idea: _____

> Laura, could I borrow your phone for a minute? The bus is late and I need to call my mom.

Useful Expressions
Making and responding to requests

Can / Could I borrow your phone?
    (= Is it OK if I borrow...)
Can / Could you lend me your phone?
    (= Would you please lend...)

Positive responses	Negative response
Sure. No problem. Certainly.	I'm sorry, but... (+ reason).

Speaking tip
May I... is more polite than *Can / Could I...*: *May I borrow your pen for a second?*

D 👥 Change roles and create a new conversation.

5 GRAMMAR

A Turn to page 73. Complete the exercise. Then do **B–E** below.

Like to	Would like to
Sentence 1: I **like to** spend time in the Outback.	*Sentence 2:* I**'d like to** spend time in the Outback.

B  Read the sentences. Which ones are logical follow-up statements to Sentence 1 above? Which ones could follow Sentence 2? Why? Discuss your answers with a partner.

a. I always enjoy my time there.

b. I hope to go someday.

c. It looks like a beautiful place.

d. I'm planning to go again next year.

e. It's a lot of fun.

f. People say it's a lot of fun.

C Read the questions. Then circle the correct words to complete each answer.

1. What do you usually do on the weekend?

   I like to / I'd like to relax.

2. Why are you studying for the TOEFL exam?

   I like to / I'd like to find a job overseas.

3. What's your New Year's resolution?

   I like to / I'd like to get in shape.

4. Why is Mike gaining weight?

   He likes to / He'd like to eat desserts.

5. How was your trip to Brazil?

   We loved it! We like to / We'd like to visit again.

6. Do your parents both work?

   Yes, but they like to / they'd like to retire soon.

D Write sentences about yourself. Use these topics and start each sentence with *I like to* or *I'd like to*.

1. your free time

2. after graduation

3. your favorite TV show

4. fun things you do in your city

5. plans for next summer

6. changes in your life

E  Take turns talking about your answers in **D** with a partner.

The Australian Outback

6 COMMUNICATION

A   Look at the lists of bad habits and bad qualities below. Add one more idea to each list. Tell your partner.

BAD HABITS	BAD QUALITIES
I…	I'm…
bite my nails.	messy.
spend too much money.	lazy.
eat a lot of junk food.	late all the time.
talk on the phone too much.	careless with money.
watch too much TV.	too laid-back.
your idea: _____	your idea: _____

> **i** A **habit** is something you do regularly: *I check my email when I get up.* A **quality** is something that describes your personality: *I'm a serious student.*

B   Look at the pictures with a partner. What bad habits and bad qualities do these people have?

C   **Student A:** Imagine that you are the person in Picture 1 above. First, tell your partner about your bad habits and bad qualities. Then tell your partner how you want to change. Ask your partner for advice.

Student B: Listen to your partner. Suggest ways that he or she can change.

A: I like to go shopping, but I spend too much money.

B: You should try to save some money—a little bit each month.

A: I'd like to save money, but I have a lot of bills. What can I do?

B: Well, don't use your credit cards. It's…

D   Switch roles and do another role play. **Student B** is the person in Picture 2 above.

Rina, Nick, and Sarah are graduating from college.

1 VOCABULARY

A 🔁 Look at the photo and read the students' comments below. Answer the questions with a partner.

> *Rina:* I'm **getting ready** to graduate next week. I **applied for** four jobs, but so far… nothing. I know **it takes time**, but I want to get a job soon.
>
> *Nick:* My **goal** is to **become** a doctor. So I'm going to go to medical school after graduation.
>
> *Sarah:* I'm so glad school is over! I want to **take it easy**. I'm going to **take** the summer **off** and travel.

1. What are all the students getting ready to do?

2. Whose goal is to:

   a. go back to school? _____

   b. get a job? _____

   c. relax and not work? _____

B 🔁 Complete the sentences about yourself. Then tell a partner your answers.

1. I'm getting ready to _____ soon.

2. This summer, I plan to _____.

   a. take it easy   c. travel

   b. work or study   d. other: _____

3. After I finish school, my goal is to _____.

   a. take a month off and do nothing   c. travel

   b. apply for jobs   d. other: _____

4. It takes _____ year(s) to graduate from college in my country.

Word Bank

get ready = prepare (to do something)

take it easy = relax

take (time) off = stop working

ℹ️ **It takes** + time expression + infinitive

It takes time <u>to get</u> a job.

It took four years <u>to finish</u> college.

> I'm getting ready to take the TOEFL soon.

2 LISTENING

A 🔄 Who is your favorite singer? What did he or she do in the last couple of months? Check (✓) the boxes. Then tell a partner.

☐ went on tour   ☐ appeared on TV

☐ recorded an album   ☐ your idea: _____

B 🔊 **Listen for details.** Listen to the interview with Yeliz, a singer. Circle the correct words to complete the sentences. **Track 19**

1. Yeliz is in Los Angeles / Istanbul now. She lives in Istanbul / Scotland.

2. She hardly ever / often travels.

3. Yeliz is getting ready to take time off / put out a new album.

4. Then in two months, she plans to take it easy / go on tour.

5. Yeliz plans to / doesn't plan to quit singing in school.

C 🔊 **Understand a speaker's attitude.** Listen again. How does Yeliz feel about these things? Circle your answers and write one key word that supports each answer. **Track 19**

How does Yeliz feel about...

1. traveling?   She likes / doesn't like it.   key word: _____

2. recording?   She likes / doesn't like it.   key word: _____

3. school?   She likes / doesn't like it.   key word: _____

D 🔄 Do you think Yeliz's life is interesting? Why or why not? Tell a partner.

A 🔄 **Make predictions.** Look at the title of the reading and the photo. Guess: What are these people's future goals? Tell a partner. Then read the passage to check your ideas.

B **Read for details.** Read the passage again and complete the chart.

	Wang	Hicham
1. Where does he or she live?		
2. What does he or she do?		
3. What is his or her goal?		
4. What's stopping him or her?		

C **Scan for information.** Quickly find each of the activities below in the reading. Is the person doing it now? Check *N*. Is it the person's future goal? Check *F*. Underline the sentence in the reading that helped you choose your answer.

Yi Wang

1. teach at a university   N ☐   F ☐
2. write a film   N ☐   F ☐
3. go to film festivals   N ☐   F ☐

Hicham Nassir

4. live in London   N ☐   F ☐
5. play professional soccer   N ☐   F ☐
6. practice every day   N ☐   F ☐

D 🔄 Role-play a dialog between Wang and Hicham. Ask the questions in **B**. At the end, give some advice: How can the person make his or her goal happen?

> Hi, I'm Yi Wang.

> Hi, I'm Hicham Nassir.

> Where are you from, Hicham?

> I'm from Sudan.

A LIFETIME
DREAM

A high school student from Sudan and a teacher from China tell about their hopes for the future.

Hicham Nassir

Seventeen-year-old Hicham Nassir is getting ready for a soccer match with his teammates. Hicham, a student and his school's best player, is a native of Sudan. He now lives in London with his family.

"My parents are worried. They want me to go to college and major in business or law," he explains. "They want me to get a job as a lawyer or work as a businessman. I understand them, but I want to become a pro soccer player. This summer, I'm going to practice really hard every day."

And what about his parents? "I hope they change their minds,"[1] says Hicham. "I want to play soccer professionally. It's my dream."

Yi Wang

"At the moment, I'm teaching chemistry at a university in Beijing. It's a good job, but my dream is to make films," says 29-year-old Yi Wang. "In China, young artists move to Beijing from all over the country. Many of them are painters, writers, and actors. I'd like to take some time off and make a film about their lives and their work."

Wang is writing a film now with help from her friends. But it isn't easy. "At the moment, the biggest problem is money," explains Wang. "We don't have much."

But this isn't going to stop Wang and her partners. They are ambitious. "First, we're going to make this movie. Then we'd like to show it in China and, maybe someday, at film festivals around the world. It's going to take time, but I think we can do it."

[1]If you *change your mind,* you change your opinion about something.

4 GRAMMAR See page 82 for practice with the present continuous for future tense.

A Turn to page 74. Complete the exercises. Then do **B** and **C** below.

The Future with *be going to*				
Subject + *be*	**(*not*)**	***going to***	**Verb**	**Future time expression**
I'm	(not)	**going to**	start	college	this fall. / in August. next month. / after graduation.

***Yes / No* and *Wh-* questions**						**Answers**	
	Are	you	**going to**	start	college?	Yes, I am.	No, I'm not.
When	are					(I'm going to start) in August.	

B Answer the questions in the chart by checking (✓) the correct box for each. Then add one more.

In the future, are you going to...	Yes, I am.	Maybe.	Probably not.	No, I'm not.
study English?				
take the TOEFL exam?				
move to another city?				
get married?				
apply for a job?				
visit another country?				
learn another language?				
start your own business?				
take time off?				
_____?				

C Take turns asking and answering the questions in **B** with a partner. Then ask one follow-up *Wh-* question with *be going to.* Use the models below.

A: In the future, are you going to move to another city?

B: Yes, maybe.

A: Really? Where are you going to move?

B: Tokyo. I want to get a job there.

A: Are you going to move to another city?

B: Probably not.

A: Why not?

B: I like my hometown. It's comfortable here.

5 WRITING

A Read about one person's goal. Notice the words in bold used to introduce new topics. Then answer the questions below.

My Goal

My goal is to run in the São Paulo International Marathon next year. I'm going to do three things to get ready. **First**, I'm going to buy some new shoes. I need good shoes for running. **Also**, I'm going to run every day for ten months. A marathon is 42 kilometers, and a runner needs a lot of practice. **Finally**, I'm going to quit eating junk food and start eating more fruit and vegetables. A runner needs to be healthy. It's going to be hard, but I can do it!

1. What is the person's goal?

2. He is going to do three things to make his goal happen. What are they?

ℹ The writer explains each of his three ideas with an extra sentence.

B What is one of your goals? Complete the sentences with your ideas. Then use your notes to write a paragraph.

My goal is to…

To do this, first, I'm going to…

Also, I'm going to…

Finally, I'm going to…

It's going to be hard, but I'm going to do it!

C 🔁 Exchange papers with a partner.

1. Answer questions 1 and 2 in **A** about your partner.

2. Circle any mistakes in your partner's writing. Then return the paper to him or her.

The São Paulo International Marathon

6 COMMUNICATION

A 🔁 Prepare a short talk.

1. Practice with a partner: Use your notes in Writing to talk about your goal. Do not just read your paragraph.

2. Find photos or a video clip to use in your presentation.

B 👥 Work in a small group. Give your presentation.

1. When you listen, answer questions 1 and 2 in Writing **A**.

2. Can the speaker do anything else to make his or her goal happen? Tell the group.

4 SHOPPING

Look at the photo. Answer the questions.

1 Is there a shopping mall in your city? What is it called?

2 Do you ever go to these kinds of stores?
- a department store
- a clothing store
- a coffee shop
- a supermarket

3 What are the stores' names? What do you buy there?

UNIT GOALS

1 Identify common foods

2 Talk about things you need

3 Describe your shopping habits

4 Discuss different places to shop and what they sell

A luxury shopping mall in Berlin, Germany

Farmers' markets are growing around the world. This one is in Otavalo, Ecuador.

1 **VIDEO** Field of Greens

A Look at the photo. What do you see? Do you have any markets like this in your city?

B ▶ 🔄 Watch the video. What fruits and vegetables do you see? Make a list in your notebook. Compare your list to a partner's.

C ▶ Watch the video again. Then answer the questions.

1. What is unusual about the first farm in the video?

2. Do farmers' markets sell foods besides *produce* (fruits and vegetables)?

3. What are the main benefits of shopping at farmers' markets?

D 🔄 With a partner, plan a dinner menu. Use foods that you can find at a farmers' market. Share your menu with the class. Which pair has the best menu?

2 VOCABULARY

Word Bank

Word partnerships

fresh / frozen / junk **food**

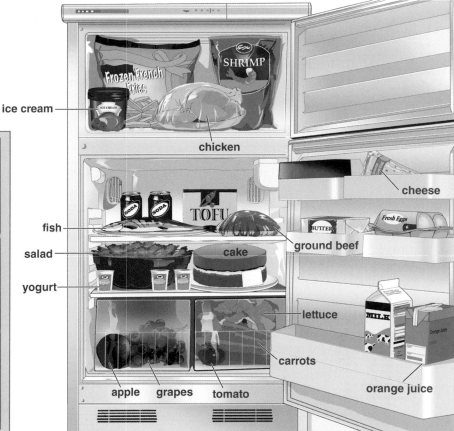

ice cream

chicken

cheese

fish

ground beef

salad

cake

yogurt

lettuce

carrots

bananas

apple   grapes   tomato   orange juice

A 🔄 Practice saying the items in the picture with a partner. Which of these foods do you eat? Tell your partner.

B 🔄 Work with your partner. On a piece of paper, copy the chart below. Think of examples for each type of food. Use words from the picture and your own ideas.

Fresh foods	Frozen foods	Junk foods	Breakfast foods	Foods you eat every day

C 🔄 Share your chart with another pair. Then ask and answer these questions.

1. What is one thing in your chart that isn't in the picture above?
2. Which items in your chart do you like? Are there any items you *don't* like to eat or drink?

3 LISTENING

A 🔊 **Pronunciation: Syllables.** Practice saying the words aloud. Then listen and repeat. **Track 21**

1. fish   2. soda   3. potato

B 🔊 🔄 **Pronunciation: Syllables.** Work with a partner. Read each word aloud. How many syllables does it have: one, two, or three? Guess. Then listen and check your answers. **Track 22**

	1	2	3		1	2	3
1. milk	☐	☐	☐	6. cake	☐	☐	☐
2. carrots	☐	☐	☐	7. yogurt	☐	☐	☐
3. tomato	☐	☐	☐	8. apple	☐	☐	☐
4. cheese	☐	☐	☐	9. cereal	☐	☐	☐
5. banana	☐	☐	☐				

C 🔄 **Use background knowledge.** Look at the two pictures below. What's in each bag? Make two lists. Tell a partner.

D 🔊 **Listen for gist.** Listen. Which shopping bag is Allison's? Circle it. **Track 23**

E 🔊 **Listen for details.** Listen. Allison's mom changes one item on the list. Put an X on the item in the shopping bag. Write the name of the new item. **Track 24**

_____

F 🔊 **Listen for details.** How do Allison and her mom talk about the foods they need? Match the items on the left with the words on the right. Then listen and check your answers. **Track 25**

1. I need a _____ of bread.   a. bunch
2. And a _____ of lettuce.   b. head
3. A _____ of ice cream.   c. carton
4. Please get a _____ of carrots, OK? d. loaf

G 🔄 Cover your answers in **D–F** and tell a partner: What items does Allison buy for her mom?

4 SPEAKING

A 🔊 Read the conversation and listen. Underline the foods Ken and Rachel have. Circle the foods they need. **Track 26**

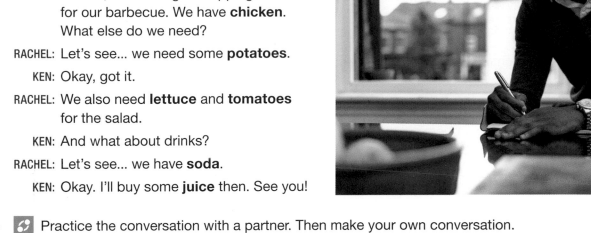

KEN: Rachel, I'm making a shopping list for our barbecue. We have **chicken**. What else do we need?

RACHEL: Let's see... we need some **potatoes**.

KEN: Okay, got it.

RACHEL: We also need **lettuce** and **tomatoes** for the salad.

KEN: And what about drinks?

RACHEL: Let's see... we have **soda**.

KEN: Okay. I'll buy some **juice** then. See you!

B 🔁 Practice the conversation with a partner. Then make your own conversation. Use your own ideas for the **bold** words.

SPEAKING STRATEGY

C Imagine you are having a class party. Everyone in the class must bring something to the party. Think of an idea and write it on the board.

D 🔁 Work with a partner. Look at the checklist below. These are things you need for the party. Look at the items on the board. Use the Useful Expressions to talk about the things you have and the things you need for your party.

<u>Class Party Checklist</u>

food

drinks

dessert

napkins, cups, plates

forks, spoons, knives, chopsticks

chairs

Useful Expressions
Talking about things you need
Do we need anything?
Yes, we do. We need soda and bottled water.
Let's see... we need...
No, we don't. We (already) have everything.
What else do we need?
We still need...
Nothing. I think we're all set.
Anything else?
Yes, we need...
No, that's it. We have everything.
Speaking tip
You can use *let's see* when you are thinking carefully about something.

E 🔼 Share your ideas in **D** with another pair.

5 GRAMMAR See pages 83-84 for more practice with count and noncount nouns.

A Turn to page 75. Complete the exercise. Then do **B–F** below.

Count and Noncount Nouns	
Count	**Noncount**
a tomato, an apple	bread, rice
two carrots, three eggs	coffee, sugar

B 🗩 Study the chart above. With a partner, write *C* or *N* to say if each phrase describes count or noncount nouns.

1. _____ can follow *a* or *an*

2. _____ can follow numbers

3. _____ are always singular

4. _____ have singular and plural forms

C Complete the sentences with *a* or *an*. If no article is needed, leave the space blank.

1. Do you want _____ rice or _____ baked potato with your dinner?

2. Billy wants _____ fruit. Give him _____ apple.

3. Do you usually put _____ sugar in _____ tea?

4. I often eat _____ banana as a snack.

5. Is there _____ salt in this soup?

6. I have _____ cereal and _____ egg every morning for breakfast.

D Read the sentences. Circle *T* for true or *F* for false. Use your own information.

1. I don't like soda because it has too much sugar.   T   F

2. I usually eat pasta once or twice a week.   T   F

3. You can usually find apples, oranges, or some
   kind of fruit in my refrigerator.   T   F

4. I eat more bread than rice.   T   F

5. I drink at least two glasses of water a day.   T   F

6. I need coffee in the morning to wake up.   T   F

7. I don't eat hot soup in the summer.   T   F

8. I eat too much cake.   T   F

E 🗩 Which nouns in **D** are count? Which are noncount? Tell a partner.

F 🗩 Compare your answers in **D** with your partner's.

> Soda has too much sugar, but I like it.

> Me too. I drink a can of soda every day.

6 COMMUNICATION

A Read about this TV show. Think about what it would be like to live on the island.

There is a new reality show on TV. On this show, people stay on an island in the Pacific Ocean for one month to win money. Here is some information about the island:

- There are a lot of fish in the ocean.

- On the island, there are a lot of coconuts and fruit trees. There's also a lot of sand!

- There's very little water to drink on the island.

- In the afternoon, it is very hot (100 degrees F / 38 degrees C).

B You want to be on the show. For your stay on the island, you can choose six items from the list below. Is there anything you want to add to the list? Write it. Then circle the six items you need.

meat	toothpaste	bananas	bandages	a knife
bottled water	soap	oranges	coffee or tea	matches
rice	sunscreen	magazines	toilet paper	_____
bread	a hat	shampoo	vitamins	_____

C Join a group of three or four people. Compare your answers. Explain your choices. Together make *one* list of six items.

> There's very little water on the island. We need to bring water.

D Explain your final list to the class.

1 VOCABULARY

	Word Bank
go shopping = shop (for something)	
Opposites	
affordable ↔ **expensive**	
buy ↔ **sell**	
credit or **debit card** ↔ **cash**	
on sale ↔ **full price**	

A Read the sentences. Review the meaning of the words in **blue** with your instructor. Then complete the sentences so they are true for you.

1. I usually **shop** for things _____.

   a. alone   b. with one person   c. with a group

2. I **buy** most of my clothes _____.

   a. online   b. at stores in **a mall**   c. in my neighborhood

3. I _____ buy things **on sale**. The price is lower, so the items are more **affordable**.

   a. often   b. sometimes   c. never

4. I **spend** _____ **money** on electronics (computers, phones) each year.

   a. a lot of   b. some   c. no

5. I **pay** for most things with _____.

   a. **cash**   b. a **debit card**   c. a **credit card**

B 🔁 Tell a partner your answers in **A**. Your partner asks you one follow-up question.

> I buy most of my clothes at stores in a mall.

> What's your favorite store?

2 LISTENING

A Look at the photos above and the list of stores below. Write the correct number (1–4) on each picture. Then write the correct letter (a–d) on each line to match the items with the stores.

Stores

1. a candy store _____
2. an electronics store _____
3. a jewelry store _____
4. a thrift store _____

Items

a. computers, phones
b. used clothes and furniture
c. chocolate
d. rings, necklaces

B 🔊 **Listen for gist.** Listen. In each conversation, the people are shopping. Where are they? Write *1, 2,* or *3*. One store is extra. **Track 27**

_____ a candy store   _____ an electronics store   _____ a jewelry store   _____ a thrift store

C 🔊 **Listen for details.** Read the sentences. Then listen again. Circle the correct answer. **Track 27**

Store 1

1. The man is shopping for _____.
   a. candy   b. a ring   c. a phone
2. The man _____.
   a. goes to another store
   b. spends a lot of money
   c. buys something affordable

Store 2

1. The _____ like(s) the store a lot.
   a. man   b. woman   c. man and woman
2. The woman says the coat is _____.
   a. expensive   b. affordable   c. on sale

Store 3

1. The items in this store are _____.
   a. expensive   b. affordable   c. on sale
2. The man pays with _____.
   a. cash   b. a credit card   c. a debit card

D 🔄 Do you ever shop at any of the places in **A**? If yes, what do you buy? Tell a partner.

3 READING 🔊 Track 28

A 🔄 **Make predictions.** Read the title. Is the article about expensive or affordable stores in Seoul? Tell a partner.

B **Identify main ideas.** Read the article. What does each paragraph (1–4) talk about? Write the words in the reading. One is extra.

Art   Books and Comics   Clothing
Electronics   Food and More

C **Scan for details.** Match the items (1–6) with the place(s) where you can buy them (a–e). Some items may have more than one answer.

1. affordable clothes _____
2. a cell phone _____
3. expensive clothes _____
4. a traditional noodle soup _____
5. souvenirs _____
6. items for the home _____

a. Dongdaemun Market
b. Gangnam
c. Insadong
d. Namdaemun Market
e. Yongsan Market

D **Scan for details.** Write a number or word next to each place. If a number or word is not given, write *NG*.

The number of...

1. department stores in Gangnam: _____
2. malls in Dongdaemun Market: _____
3. stores in Dongdaemun Market: _____
4. stores in Yongsan Market: _____
5. places to eat in Namdaemun Market: _____
6. shops in Insadong: _____

E 🔷 In your city, what are the best stores or neighborhoods to shop for the things in **B**? With a partner, make a shopping guide for visitors. Share it with the class.

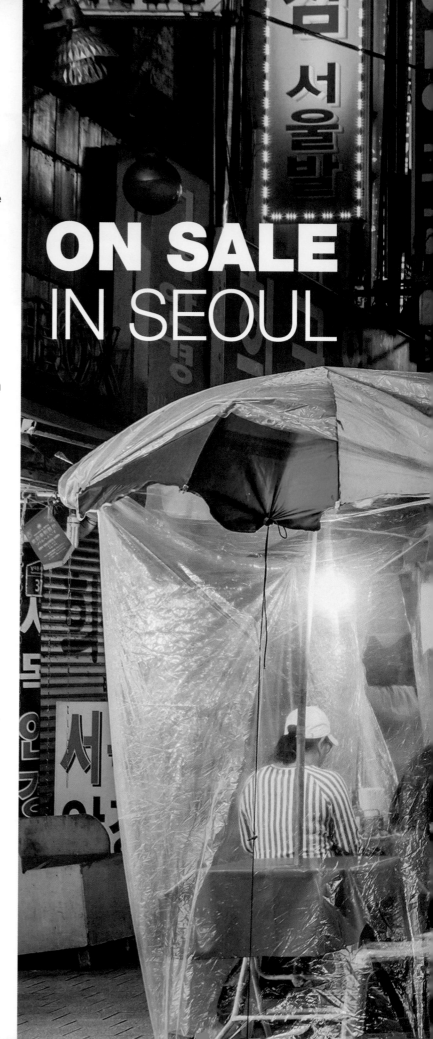

ON SALE
IN SEOUL

Are you planning to visit Seoul? South Korea's capital city has thousands of stores, so give yourself a day or more to go shopping. Here are some things you can buy:

1. _____

Need something to wear? Seoul has a lot of interesting places to shop for clothes. Department stores in the Gangnam neighborhood sell the latest fashions,[1] but they are expensive. For something more affordable, visit Dongdaemun Market. This large shopping area has over 20 malls and more than 25,000 smaller stores. Remember to bring cash and a shopping bag to hold all your items!

2. _____

Yongsan Market is the place to go for a new computer, phone, or camera. It has 5,000 stores and many items are on sale.

[1] *The latest fashions* are the most popular clothes of a certain time.
[2] A *souvenir* is something you buy on a trip to remember a place.

3. _____

Like Dongdaemun, Namdaemun Market is very large and has a lot of shops. These shops sell clothing, items for the home, and many other things—all at affordable prices. Namdaemun is also famous for its food, and there are many places to eat. Most sell traditional Korean dishes, including *kalguksu*—a delicious noodle soup.

4. _____

Looking for a souvenir[2] to take home? Visit Insadong, a beautiful, old neighborhood. Many shops sell traditional Korean drawings and other kinds of art. Some items are expensive, but many are affordable.

Outdoor food stalls like this one are common in Namdaemun.

4 GRAMMAR

A Turn to page 76. Complete the exercises. Then do **B–D** below.

Quantifiers with Affirmative and Negative Statements			
	Count nouns		**Noncount nouns**
	Do you have **any** friends?		Do you have **any** money?
Affirmative	Yes, I have **a lot of** / **many** friends. **some** friends.		Yes, I have **a lot of** money. **some** money.
Negative	No, I don't have **a lot of** / **many** friends. **any** friends.		No, I don't have **a lot of** / **much** money. **any** money.

B Make the sentences true for you. Circle a verb and then use a quantifier.

1. I (buy) / don't buy ____a lot of____ clothing online.
2. I have / don't have _____ expensive shoes.
3. I wear / don't wear _____ jewelry.
4. I read / don't read _____ magazines.
5. I drink / don't drink _____ soda.
6. I spend / don't spend _____ money on souvenirs when I travel.
7. I have / don't have _____ video games at home.
8. I buy / don't buy _____ music online.

C 🔄 Ask a partner about his or her answers in **B**. Ask a question with *any.* Then ask one follow-up question. Are you and your partner similar or different?

> Do you buy any clothing online?

> No, I like to try things on.

D 👥 Share one way you and your partner are alike and one way you are different with the class.

5 WRITING

A 🔄 Read the paragraph. Answer the questions with a partner.

1. Where is the writer's favorite place to shop?
2. What kind of store is it?
3. Why is this store her favorite? Give two reasons.

> My favorite place to shop is Uniqlo. It is a popular clothing store. I like this store for two reasons. **First**, a lot of their clothes are affordable. In a department store, I can only buy one pair of jeans. At Uniqlo, I can buy two or three. And the store always has things on sale! I'm a student and I don't have much money, so this is important. **Second**, Uniqlo's clothes are casual but nice. Many things are good for school and work. **For these reasons**, Uniqlo is my favorite place to shop.

B Answer the questions in **A** about your favorite place to shop. For each reason you give, explain it with an extra sentence or two. Then use your notes and the example to help you write your own paragraph.

C 🔁 Exchange your writing with a partner. Read his or her paragraph.

1. Are there any mistakes? If yes, circle them.

2. Answer the questions in **A** about your partner's writing. Do you know this store? Do you like it? Why or why not?

3. Return the paper to your partner. Make corrections to your own paragraph.

6 COMMUNICATION

A 🔁 Read about Jessie. Then describe her apartment with a partner.

Jessie is a 22-year-old university exchange student. She's living in your country for one year. She lives in a small apartment near her school. This is her apartment.

> Jessie doesn't have much furniture.

B 🔁 Jessie's parents want to visit her. Help Jessie prepare for her parents' visit. Work with a partner.

- What does her apartment have?
- What does her apartment need? Make a list.
- Where can she buy these things? Put your ideas on the list.

Things Jessie needs	Place to shop

> She needs some chairs. She can buy them at a department store.

C 🔼 Compare your list with another pair's list.

1 STORYBOARD

A Rolf is telling Brigit about his trip. Look at the pictures and complete the conversation. More than one answer may be possible for each blank.

B Practice the conversation with a partner. Then change roles and practice again.

2 SEE IT AND SAY IT

A 🔁 Talk about the picture with a partner. Answer these questions.

- Where are these people?
- What are they doing?
- Look at the different ads. What are they about?

Now answer these questions.

- How is the traffic and pollution in your city?
- How often do you take public transportation?
- What other forms of transportation do you take?
- Ask your partner one more question about the picture.

B 🔁 With a partner, choose one pair of people in the picture. Role-play a conversation between the two people.

3 THEY'RE GOING TO GET MARRIED!

A Look at the wedding announcement below. Two people are getting married. Think of a man and a woman. They can be famous people or other people you know. Complete the information about them.

We're Getting Married!

Name: Name:

Job: Job:

Age: Age:

Personality: Personality:

B Work alone. You are going to interview the man and woman in **A** using the questions below. Read the questions and complete the last three with *be going to*.

- When did you meet?
- How did you meet?
- When are you going to get married?
- Who are you going to invite to the wedding?
- Where _____?
- How much _____?
- How many _____?

C Conduct the interview with a partner.

Student A: You are one of the people in **A**. Answer the reporter's questions. Use your imagination.

Student B: You are a newspaper reporter. Use your questions to interview the man or woman. Take notes.

D Switch roles and do the interview again. **Student A** is now the reporter and **Student B** is one of the people in **A**.

E Share some of your interview notes with another pair.

> I interviewed Bruno Mars. He's dating Mia, our classmate! They're going to get married next month!

> Really? How did they meet?

4 LISTENING

A 🔊 Look at each photo. Then listen to the four sentences for each one. Circle the letter of the sentence that best describes the photo. **Track 29**

1.

A   B   C   D

2.

A   B   C   D

3.

A   B   C   D

4.

A   B   C   D

5 STORYBOARD

A Leo and Emma are having lunch in the cafeteria. Look at the pictures and complete the conversations. More than one answer is possible for each blank.

B Practice the conversations with a partner. Then change roles and practice again.

6 SEE IT AND SAY IT

A 🗣 Talk about the picture with a partner.

- What's happening in the scene?
- Who looks surprised? bored? excited?
- What kind of movie is it?

B 👥 Get into a group of three or four people. You are going to perform the movie scene in the picture.

1. Discuss the scene. What's happening? Why do you think it's happening?
2. Choose a person in the scene to role-play.
3. Create a short role play of six to eight sentences. Practice it with your group.

C 👥 Perform your scene for the class.

7 TIMES CHANGE

A Look at the activities in the chart. Add one more idea. Complete the chart for yourself. Check (✓) the things you can do now and the things you knew how to do five years ago.

	Me		Partner 1		Partner 2	
	Now	5 years ago	Now	5 years ago	Now	5 years ago
drive						
speak a second language						
cook simple dishes						
your idea: _____						

B Ask two classmates about the activities. Use *can* and *know how to* in your questions.

A: Can you drive?

B: Yes, I can. I passed the test last year.

A: Did you know how to drive five years ago?

B: No, I didn't. I was too young to drive.

C Look at the information in your chart. Which partner are you more similar to? Tell the class.

8 LISTENING

A Look at the pictures. Do these things ever happen where you live? Tell a partner.

☐ how to survive a tornado ☐ how to survive an earthquake ☐ how to survive a house fire

B Listen. Tom is talking to a group of students. What are they talking about? Check (✓) the correct answer above. **Track 30**

C What rules do you think Tom is going to say? Make predictions. Then listen to the full conversation. Check (✓) the correct answers. **Track 31**

☐ Open the windows.

☐ Get under a desk.

☐ Go to the store for food and water.

☐ Don't stand near the windows.

☐ Go outdoors and stand in the street.

☐ Don't use matches.

D Have you ever been in an earthquake, a fire, a tornado, or a bad storm? Tell your partner what happened.

> Two years ago, there was a big storm. It was scary. We couldn't leave the house.

9 PLANS FOR THE DAY

A You are going to make an imaginary schedule for tomorrow. Write five activities from the box on the daily planner below.

30 minutes	1 hour	1½ hours	2 hours
go grocery shopping	go to the library	clean your apartment	do your homework
get a haircut	do research on the Internet	work out at the gym	meet a friend for coffee

10:00 AM _____

10:30 AM _____

11:00 AM _____

11:30 AM _____

12:00 PM _____

12:30 PM _____

1:00 PM _____

1:30 PM _____

2:00 PM _____

2:30 PM _____

3:00 PM _____

3:30 PM _____

4:00 PM _____

4:30 PM _____

5:00 PM _____

5:30 PM _____

6:00 PM _____

6:30 PM _____

7:00 PM _____

7:30 PM _____

8:00 PM _____

8:30 PM _____

B 🗣 Think of a fun activity. Then invite your partner to join you. Agree on a good time and write the activity in your daily planner.

A: What are you doing at 2:00 tomorrow?

B: I'm getting a haircut.

A: How about at 3:00?

B: Nothing. I'm free.

A: Great. Do you want to see a movie?

B: Sure, I'd love to!

C 🗣 Think of a different fun activity and invite a new partner to join you.

UNIT 1 ALL ABOUT YOU

LESSON A

Vocabulary

play...
badminton
baseball
basketball
hockey
ping pong
soccer
tennis
volleyball

cards
darts
golf
rugby

do...
judo
pilates
yoga

gymnastics
crafts
kickboxing
puzzles

go...
bowling
jogging
skiing
surfing
swimming

camping
climbing
fishing
golfing

Speaking Strategy

Inviting with *Do you want*
Do you want to come?
  [*want* + *to* + verb]
  Sure, I'd love to!
  Sorry, I can't. I'm busy.
  Um, no thanks. I'm not
    good at...

Offering with *Do you want*
Do you want some ice cream?
  [*want* + noun]
  Yes, please. / Yes, thanks.
  No, thank you. / No, thanks.
    I'm fine.

LESSON B

Vocabulary

ambitious ↔ **laid-back** / relaxed
bright / intelligent
careful ↔ **careless**
competitive
creative
generous ↔ **selfish**
impulsive ↔ **careful**
organized ↔ **messy**
patient ↔ impatient
private
shy
talkative ↔ **reserved**
workaholic

UNIT 2 THE MIND

LESSON A

Vocabulary

bring back memories
can (sing) **from memory**
forget / remember (to do my
    homework / my house key)
forget / remember (+ noun)
good at remembering
I'll never forget the day...
have a(n) (**excellent / sharp /
    good / bad / poor**) **memory**
a (**happy / good / sad / painful**)
    memory

Speaking Strategy

**Expressing degrees
    of certainty**
Are they in your backpack?
    Yes, they are. / No, they aren't.
        (very certain)
    I think so. / I don't think so.
        (less certain)
    Maybe. I'm not sure. (not very
        certain)
    I have no idea. (don't know)

LESSON B

Vocabulary

(**be**) **asleep** ↔ (**be**) **awake**
fall asleep ↔ **wake up**
go to bed ↔ **stay up** (**late**)
get up ↔ **stay in bed**

dream
nightmare

UNIT 3 CHANGE

LESSON A

Vocabulary

**be in bad shape / be out
    of shape**
be in good shape
find / get a (**new**) **job**
gain weight ↔ **lose weight**
lose a job
make / earn (**more / less**) **money**
start exercising
stop / quit smoking

(New Year's) resolution
(good, bad) habit
(good, bad) quality

Speaking Strategy

**Making and responding
    to requests**
Can / Could I borrow your phone?
Can / Could you lend me your
    phone?

Positive responses
Sure. No problem.
Certainly.

Negative response
I'm sorry, but... (+ reason).

LESSON B

Vocabulary

apply for (a job)
become (something)
get ready (to do something)
goal
it takes time
prepare
relax
stop working
take it easy
take (time) **off**

UNIT 4 SHOPPING

LESSON A

Vocabulary

apple
(a bunch of) **bananas**
(ground) **beef**
(a loaf of) **bread**
butter
(a piece of) **cake**
(a bunch of) **carrots**
(a box of) **cereal**
cheese
chicken
coffee
chips
(a carton of) **eggs**
fish
(a bunch of) **grapes**
(a carton of) **ice cream**
(a head of) **lettuce**
milk
noodles
(orange) **juice**
rice
salad
(a can of) **soda**
soup
sugar
tea
tofu
tomato
yogurt

fresh / frozen / junk **food**

Speaking Strategy

Talking about things you need
Do we need anything?
   Yes, we do. We need soda
     and bottled water.
     Let's see… we need…
   No, we don't. We (already) have
     everything.
What else do we need?
   We still need…
   Nothing. I think we're all set.
Anything else?
   Yes, we need…
   No, that's it. We have
     everything.

LESSON B

Vocabulary

affordable ↔ **expensive**
buy ↔ **sell**
cash
credit card
debit card
full price
go shopping
mall
on sale
pay
shop (*for* something / *at*
   a place)
shop / **spend** (**money**)

UNIT **1** ALL ABOUT YOU

LESSON A

Verb + Infinitive	
I **love** <u>to play</u> volleyball. I **forgot** <u>to explain</u> the rules. Can you **learn** <u>to surf</u> in one summer?	The infinitive is *to* + the base form of the verb. It can follow these common verbs: *forget, hate, learn, like, love, need, decide, plan, prepare,* and *want*.

Verb + Noun	
I **like** <u>most sports</u>. I'**m planning** <u>a big trip</u>. We **prepared** <u>dinner</u> for everyone.	All the verbs above can also be followed by a noun or noun phrase.

A Use the verb in parentheses to complete each sentence with the verb + *to* or the verb alone. (Some of the verbs may be in the simple past tense.)

1. I (want) _____ go camping next weekend.

2. Don't (forget) _____ explain the rules.

3. Do you (hate) _____ gym class?

4. I have a silver medal, and now I (want) _____ a gold one.

5. You (need) _____ stretch before you do pilates.

6. I can't go swimming because I (forget) _____ my swimsuit.

7. I'm serious about ping pong. I (hate) _____ lose.

8. I (learn) _____ a new game. Do you want me to show you?

LESSON B

How often...? Frequency Expressions			
How often do you see your best friend?	(I see her)	**every**	day / Monday / week / month / summer.
		once **twice** **three times** **several times**	a day / a week / a month / a year.
		all the time. (= very often) *I see her all the time.* **once in a while.** (= sometimes) *I see her once in a while.* **hardly ever.*** (= almost never) *I hardly ever see her.* **never.** (= not ever)* *I never see her.*	

How often asks about the frequency of an event.

*Frequency expressions usually come at the end of a sentence, but it's more common for *hardly ever* and *never* to come before the verb: *"I **hardly ever** <u>see</u> her." "I **never** <u>see</u> my best friend."*

To say something never happens, you can also say: *Never.*

A 🔄 Find the mistake in each dialog and correct it. Then practice the dialogs with a partner.

1. A: How often you play tennis?

   B: Every Sunday.

2. A: How often do you wash your hair?

   B: Once a week, on Monday and Friday.

3. A: Is the bus usually on time?

   B: No, it's all the time late.

4. A: How often does Maria see her brother?

   B: Hardly ever she sees him. He works in the UK.

B Look at Ricardo's weekly schedule. Answer the questions with a word or phrase in **bold** in the chart.

Monday	Tuesday	Wednesday	Thursday	Friday	Saturday	Sunday
Class: 9–12 Work: 1–4	Work: 10–2	Class: 9–12 Work: 1–4	Work: 10–2	Class: 9–12 Work: 1–4	Study group: 10–12 Work: 1–4	Work: 3–6

How often does Ricardo...

1. have class?

2. work?

3. work from 10 to 2?

4. work from 1 to 4?

5. meet with his study group?

Answer

1a. _three times_ a week.

1b. ____on____ Monday, Wednesday, and Friday.

2a. _____ day.

2b. _____ time.

3a. _____ a week.

3b. _____ Tuesday and Thursday.

4a. _____ a week.

4b. _____ Monday, Wednesday, Friday, and Saturday.

5a. _____ .

5b. _____ .

UNIT 2 THE MIND

LESSON A

The Simple Past: Affirmative and Negative Statements (Irregular Verbs)			
Subject	***did + not***	**Verb**	
I / You / He / She / We / They		forgot	her birthday.
	didn't	forget	

- In affirmative statements, do not add -ed to form irregular past tense verbs. See the chart below for the simple past tense form of many common irregular verbs.
- In negative statements, use did not or didn't + the base form of the verb.

Present	Past	Present	Past	Present	Past	Present	Past	Present	Past
begin	began	drink	drank	give	gave	meet	met	sing	sang
bring	brought	eat	ate	go	went	pay	paid	speak	spoke
buy	bought	fall	fell	have	had	read	read*	take	took
choose	chose	feel	felt	know	knew	run	ran	teach	taught
come	came	forget	forgot	leave	left	say	said	think	thought
do	did	get	got	make	made	see	saw	wear	wore

*Note: There is a vowel shift in the past tense pronunciation of read. The vowel goes from /i/ to /ɛ/.

A Complete the story with the simple past form of the verbs in parentheses. Most of the verbs are irregular. Which ones are regular?

A Scary Memory

There (1. be) _____ a fire one day when I (2. be) _____ at school. It (3. begin) _____ around lunchtime. Soon, we all (4. smell) _____ smoke. Someone (5. say) _____ in a loud voice, "Fire!" Then the fire alarm (6. ring) _____. As we (7. walk) _____ down the hallway, I (8. feel) _____ the heat from the fire. We (9. not say) _____ anything—everyone was so quiet.

The fire truck (10. come) _____ quickly. The firefighters (11. run) _____ into the building and (12. stop) _____ the fire. After 30 minutes, we (13. go) _____ back into our school. Luckily, there (14. not be) _____ much damage. I will never forget that day.

B 🗣 Take turns reading the story in **A** with a partner. Then explain the story in your own words. Can you retell it from memory?

LESSON B

The Simple Past Tense: *Yes / No* Questions				
Did	**Subject**	**Verb**		**Short answers**
Did	you he / she / it they	stay up late wake up	last night?	Yes, I did. / No, I didn't. Yes, he did. / No, he didn't. Yes, they did. / No, they didn't.

- To ask a past tense *Yes / No* question, use *did* + subject + base form of the verb.
- Short answers are the same for both regular and irregular verbs.

The Simple Past Tense: *Wh-* Questions				
***Wh-* word**	***did***	**Subject**	**Verb**	**Answers**
When	did	you he / she / it they	study?	(I / She / They studied) last night.
			get up?	(I / She / They got up) at 7:00.
What			happened to you?	I woke up late this morning.

A Circle the mistake in each dialog and correct it.

1. A: Did Mario stayed up late last night?

   B: Yes, he did.

2. A: Did you forget your keys?

   B: No, I didn't forgot them.

3. A: Where did Julie went on her vacation?

   B: She went to Mexico.

4. A: What did happen to Yu and Amy?

   B: They slept late and missed the bus.

B Complete the dialogs with a past tense *Yes / No* or *Wh-* question or short answer.

1. A: _____ last night?

   B: I went to bed at 10:00.

2. A: _____ well?

   B: No, I didn't sleep well. I had nightmares.

3. A: _____ before bed?

   B: No, _____. I never drink coffee before bed.

C 🔁 Practice the conversations in **B** with a partner.

UNIT 3 CHANGE

LESSON A

Like to Versus Would like to						
Do		**like**	**Infinitive**			
	I					in the Outback.
		like	to spend	time		
Do	you					there?

Use *like* + the infinitive form to talk about the present.

	Would		**like**	**Infinitive**			
I	**would***						in the Outback.
			like	to spend	time		
	Would	you					there?

*It's common to use the contracted form: *I'd like to spend time in the Outback.*

Use *would like* + the infinitive form to talk about a future hope or desire.

Contractions

I'd = I would
you'd = you would
he'd = he would
she'd = she would
we'd = we would
they'd = they would

A Use the words in the box to complete the conversations. Then practice them with a partner.

I like	do you like	I'd like
I don't like	do you like	I'd like
I'd like	would you like	you'd like

A: This menu looks interesting. (1.) _____ to try something new, but I can't decide.

B: Well, what kind of food (2.) _____?

A: Let's see... (3.) _____ anything too strange... and (4.) _____ spicy food.

B: Then I think (5.) _____ the red curry. It's really spicy... and very delicious!

A: It sounds good. I think (6.) _____ that.

A: What changes (7.) _____ to make in the new year?

B: Well, for one, (8.) _____ to lose some weight. I'm out of shape.

A: I see... and, (9.) _____ to exercise?

B: Yes, I do, actually. I started exercising last month.

A: Come with me to the gym tomorrow, then. We can work out together.

The Future with *be going to*						
Subject	***be***	**(*not*)**	***going to***	**Base form**		**Future time expression**
I	**am**					tomorrow.
You	**are**					this fall.
He / She	**is**	(*not*)	**going to**	start	college	in August.
We / You / They	**are**					next week / month / year.
						after graduation.

Use *be going to* to talk about future plans.

You can also use it to make predictions: *She's going to be a great doctor.*

When the subject is a pronoun, it's common to use a contraction with *be*: *I'm going to start college...*

With a noun + *be going to*, we often say the contraction: *My sister's going to take some time off.*

Don't use the contraction in formal writing.

Yes / No questions						**Short answers**	
Is	she					Yes, she is.	No, she's not. / No, she isn't.
Are	you	**going to**	start	college	this fall?	Yes, I am.	No, I'm not.
	they					Yes, they are.	No, they're not. / No they aren't.

Wh- questions						**Answers**
When	is	he	**going to**	start	college?	(He's / I'm going to start college) in August.
	are	you				

A Complete the sentences about a student's summer plans with the correct form of *be going to.*

I (1. visit) _____ Europe after graduation. My brother (2. stay) _____ home. He (3. not travel) _____ anywhere. He (4. take) _____ it easy. My parents (5. take) _____ a week off from work. They (6. meet) _____ me in Paris. We (7. not return) _____ home until September 5.

B Complete the conversation using questions and answers with *be going to.*

JO: So, (1. when / you / leave) _____ for Europe?

NEIL: Next month.

JO: (2. you / go) _____ alone?

NEIL: No, (3. my roommate / come) _____ with me.

JO: (4. Where / you / start) _____ your trip?

NEIL: First, (5. we / fly) _____ to London. Then (6. I / visit) _____ two more cities alone.

JO: (7. your / parents / visit) _____ you in Europe?

NEIL: Yes, (8. they / meet) _____ me in Paris.

C In your notebook, write three *be going to* questions to ask about your partner's summer plans. Then interview your partner.

UNIT **4** SHOPPING

LESSON A

Count Nouns		Noncount Nouns		
Singular	**Plural**			
apple	apples	beef	bread	English divides nouns into things we can count (count nouns) and things we can't (noncount nouns). Count nouns have singular and plural forms.
carrot	carrots	cereal	cheese	
tomato	tomatoes	rice	soda	

Singular and Plural Count Nouns; Noncount Nouns					
	Article	**Noun**	**Verb**		
Singular count nouns	A	banana	is	a good snack.	Use *a / an* or *the* before the noun.
	The	banana	is	in the bowl.	Use a singular form of the verb.
Plural count nouns	—	Bananas	are	good for you.	Use *the* or no article before the noun.
	The	bananas	are	on the table.	Use a plural form of the verb.
Noncount nouns	—	Bread	is	inexpensive.	Use *the* or no article before the noun.
	The	bread	is	in the bag.	Use a singular form of the verb.

Partitives: Talking about Specific Amounts							
General amount			**Specific amount**				
Please buy	some	bread.	Please buy	a	loaf	of	bread.
		lettuce.			head		lettuce.
		ice cream.			carton		eggs.
		carrots.			bunch		grapes.

a bottle of water	a glass of juice / water	a cup of coffee / soup
a can of soup / soda	a piece of cake / chocolate	a slice of bread / pie

A Read this recipe for beef stir fry. Circle the count nouns. Underline the noncount ones.

Pour some (1.) oil into (2.) a pan and heat it up.

Add (3.) some garlic, (4.) mushrooms, and (5.) carrots into the pan and cook them.

Remove the garlic and (6.) the vegetables from the pan.

Next, cook (7.) the beef.

Put (8.) the meat and (9.) vegetables together and cover with (10.) soy sauce.

Serve over (11.) rice on (12.) a dinner plate.

Don't forget to have (13.) a drink with it!

LESSON B

	Yes / No Questions with *any*		Answers
Plural count nouns	Do you have **any**	friends?	Yes, I do.
Noncount nouns		money?	No, I don't.

Use *any* in *Yes / No* questions to ask about unknown amounts.

Quantifiers with Affirmative and Negative Statements			
		Quantifier	**Noun**
Plural count nouns	I have	a lot of / many some	friends.
	I don't have	a lot of / many any	
Noncount nouns	I have	a lot of some	money.
	I don't have	a lot of / much any	

Quantifiers give information about an amount of something.

You can answer a question with a short answer:

*Do you have **any** friends?*　　　　　*Yes, I have **a lot** (of friends).*

*Do you have **any** money?*　　　　　*No, I don't have **much** (money), just two dollars.*

Notice: *I don't have **any** friends / money. = I have **no** friends / money.*

A　Complete each sentence with the best answer.

1. Juan has $1,000,000. He has much / a lot of money.

2. Barry only has $2. He doesn't have any / much money.

3. This store only sells clothes. You can't buy any / many shoes here.

4. Rita has a lot of / many beautiful jewelry.

5. There aren't much / many department stores in this city. There are only two.

6. Leo has three friends. He has many / some friends.

B　Write a quantifier in each blank. Then practice the dialogs with a partner.

1. A: Do you have _____ questions about the homework?

   B: No, I don't have _____. I understand everything.

2. A: Are there _____ girls in this class?

   B: Yes, there are _____—three, I think.

3. A: Do you have _____ cash? I want a soda.

   B: Yes, but I don't have _____. I only have $1.

4. A: Is there _____ room in the closet for my suitcase?

   B: Yes, the closet is empty. There's _____ room.

ADDITIONAL GRAMMAR NOTES

Possessive Nouns		
Singular nouns (+ 's)	**Plural nouns (+ ')**	**Irregular plural nouns (+ 's)**
sister → sister**'s**	parents → parents**'**	children → children**'s**
brother → brother**'s**	brothers → brothers**'**	women → women**'s**

For first and last names that end in *s*, you can add **'s** or just **'**.

A Look up the word *twin* in a dictionary. Read about Hallie Parker and Annie James from the movie *The Parent Trap.* Complete the sentences with a singular noun, a plural noun, or a possessive noun.

1. Hallie Parker lives in her (father) _____ home in California, in the US.

2. Annie (James) _____ home is in London. She lives there with her (mother) _____.

3. The two (girl) _____, Hallie and Annie, are (twin) _____! But they live apart. They don't know about each other.

4. (Hallie) _____ summer plans are exciting. She's going to summer camp. And by chance, (Annie) _____ is going to the same summer camp!

5. At camp, Hallie sees her (sister) _____ face for the first time. They look the same! They are both surprised and happy.

6. Hallie doesn't know her (mom) _____ name, and Annie doesn't know her (dad) _____ name.

7. Before the two (child) _____ leave camp, they have an idea. The two (sister) _____ plan is an exciting one!

B What do you think happens next? Write three sentences. Tell your partner.

_____.

_____.

_____.

	Possessive Adjectives	Possessive Pronouns	*belong to*
Whose passport is this?	It's **my** passport. **your** **her** **his** **our** **their**	It's **mine**. **yours**. **hers**. **his**. **ours**. **theirs**.	It **belongs to me**. **you**. **her**. **him**. **us**. **them**.

Whose and *who's* have the same pronunciation but different meanings.
Whose asks about the owner of something: *Whose house is that? It's mine.*
Who's is a contraction of *Who* and *is*: *Who's studying English? Maria is.*

A Write the correct possessive pronoun for the underlined words.

1. A: That's not her suitcase.

   B: No, <u>her suitcase</u> is over there.
   hers

2. A: Can I use your cell phone? <u>My cell phone</u> doesn't work.

   B: Sorry, but I forgot my cell phone at home. Use <u>Jon's phone</u>.

3. A: Is your class fun?

   B: Yes, but <u>Aya and Leo's class</u> is more interesting.

4. A: Is your hometown hot in the summer? <u>My hometown</u> is.

   B: <u>Our hometown</u> is, too.

5. A: Your birthday is in May.

   B: That's right, and <u>your birthday</u> is in March.

B 🔊 Use the words in the chart to complete the conversation. Then practice the dialog with a partner.

JIM: Well, I have (1.) _____my_____ luggage. Where's (2.) _____ ?

BEN: Um... let's see... oh, here's (3.) _____ suitcase. No, wait... this one isn't (4.) _____ .

JIM: (5.) _____ is it?

BEN: It says Mr. Simon Konig. It belongs to (6.) _____ .

JIM: Hey, I think that man has (7.) _____ suitcase. See? He probably thinks it's (8.) _____ .

BEN: I'll ask him. Excuse me, does this suitcase belong to (9.) _____ ?

SIMON: Oh, sorry. My mistake! I thought it was (10.) _____ !

Past Forms of *be*
am / is → **was**
am not / isn't → **wasn't**
are → **were**
aren't → **weren't**

The Simple Past Tense with *be*		
Affirmative and Negative Statements		
Subject	*was / were*	
I	**was** / **wasn't**	
You	**were** / **weren't**	brave.
He / She / It	**was** / **wasn't**	
We / You / They	**were** / **weren't**	

Yes / No Questions			Answers
Was / Were	Subject		
Were	you	brave?	Yes, I **was**. / No, I **wasn't**.
	they		Yes, they **were**. / No, they **weren't**.
Was	she		Yes, she **was**. / No, she **wasn't**.
	I		Yes, you **were**. / No, you **weren't**.

Wh- Questions				Answers
Wh- word	*was / were*	Subject		
Where	**were**	you	yesterday?	At home.
When	**was**	he	in Iceland?	Two years ago.
Who	**was**	your teacher	last semester?	Ms. Hunter.

You can use these time expressions with the past tense of *be*: *yesterday*, *in 1990*, *last* semester / week, two days / years *ago*.

A 🎧 Complete the conversation with a partner. Use the correct form of the verb *be* in the past tense.

TIM: Hi, Kelly. It's Tim. I called you yesterday, but you (1. not) _____ home.

KELLY: I (2.) _____ at the library. I'm writing a paper about Pierre and Marie Curie.

TIM: They (3.) _____ scientists from France, right?

KELLY: Right. Well, actually Pierre (4.) _____ French, but his wife (5. not) _____ born in France. She (6.) _____ from Poland. She (7.) _____ also the first person to win a Nobel Prize twice.

B Complete the questions on the left. Then match them with the correct answers on the right.

1. _____ Kelly at home?
2. _____ _____ Kelly?
3. _____ the Curies scientists?
4. _____ Marie Curie born in France?
5. _____ _____ Marie Curie born?
6. _____ Marie Curie the first person to win two Nobel Prizes?
7. _____ _____ Pierre Curie from?
8. _____ _____ the Curies?

a. Yes, they were.
b. No, she wasn't.
c. No, she wasn't.
d. They were scientists.
e. Yes, she was.
f. France.
g. At the library.
h. In Poland.

The Simple Past: Affirmative and Negative Statements

I / You / He / She / We / They	visit**ed** **didn't** visit	Tokyo.
I / You / He / She / We / They	start**ed** **didn't** start	a company.

In the simple past tense, the verb form is the same for all persons.
In affirmative statements, add *–ed* or *–d*. See the spelling rules below.
In negative statements, use *did not* or *didn't* + the base form of the verb.

The Simple Past Tense of Regular Verbs: Spelling Rules

move	→	mov**ed**	If the verb ends in *e*, add *–d*.
start	→	start**ed**	If the verb ends with a consonant, add *–ed*.
stu**dy**	→	stud**ied**	If the verb ends with a consonant + *y*, change the *y* to *i* and add *–ed*.
pl**ay**	→	play**ed**	If the verb ends with a vowel + *y*, add *–ed*.
stop	→	stop**ped**	With one-syllable verbs that end with a consonant–vowel–consonant, double the last letter and add *–ed*.
fi**x**	→	fix**ed**	But do not double the last consonant if it is a *w* or *x*.
oc**cur**	→	occur**red**	With two-syllable verbs that end with a consonant–vowel–consonant, double the last consonant if the last syllable is stressed.
lis**ten**	→	listen**ed**	But do not double the last consonant if the last syllable is not stressed.

A Complete the sentences with the simple past tense of each verb. Pay attention to spelling.

1. Sanga Moses (work) _____ in a bank in the capital.

2. One day, he (visit) _____ his family.

3. He saw his sister. She (carry) _____ a lot of wood that day.

4. She (look) _____ at her brother, and she (cry) _____. She said,
   "I (not go) _____ to school today. I (walk) _____ 10 kilometers to get wood."

5. Sanga Moses (want) _____ his sister to stay in school.

6. That day, he (decide) _____ to do something. He (stop) _____ working at the bank.
   He (start) _____ Eco-Fuel Africa.

7. With a group of engineers, he (invent) _____ a new oven. It (change) _____ many
   people's lives in Uganda.

B Make sentences about things you did or didn't do yesterday. Use the verbs.

1. walk to school _____ I didn't walk to school. _____

2. text a friend _____

3. listen to a song in English _____

4. study for a test _____

5. cook dinner _____

6. watch TV _____

7. hug my mom _____

8. wash my hair _____

The Present Continuous as Future		
Subject + *be*	**Verb + *ing***	**Future time expression**
We're	seeing	a movie	today / tonight / tomorrow. in an hour. this weekend.
They're	making	next year.

You can use the present continuous tense (often with a future time expression) to talk about future plans.

Use the present continuous only when a plan exists:

Here's the plan: We're meeting downtown and then driving to the theater in my car.

Do not use the present continuous to make predictions. Use *going to* instead:

~~*He's passing the test tomorrow.*~~ *He's going to pass the test tomorrow.*

A Complete the conversation. Use the present continuous form of the verbs in parentheses and complete the time expression with the words in the box.

> Verbs that are related to movement and travel (like *go, come, take, fly, travel, visit, leave, arrive,* and *get*) are commonly used in the present continuous when expressing future time.

| in | next | this | tomorrow |

A: I'm really looking forward to summer vacation (1.) ___this___ year.

B: Why is that?

A: Because (2. I / go) _____ to Tanzania, in Africa. (3. we / leave) _____ (4.) _____ morning! I'm so excited!

B: Wow! How (5. you / get) _____ there?

A: (6. we / fly) _____ with Global Airways from New York City. And (7. we / change) _____ planes in Dubai before arriving in Dar es Salaam.

B: Do you already have a plan for the trip?

A: Yes, (8. we / visit) _____ Zanzibar for a few days and then (9. climb) _____ Mount Kilimanjaro.

B: Great! How long is the trip?

A: (10. I / stay) _____ for two weeks, so (11. I / return) _____ early (12.) _____ month. (13. my friend / travel) _____ an extra week in Africa. What about you? (14. you / go) _____ anywhere fun?

B: Not really. (15. I / visit) _____ my family down south. (16. I / drive) _____ and (17. I / leave) _____ (18.) _____ a few hours.

Count Nouns	Noncount Nouns	
This **shirt is** / These **shirts are** expensive.	This **clothing is** expensive.	Count nouns can be singular or plural. Noncount nouns are always singular.
This ring is **a dollar** / **two dollars**.	I want to save **money**. (Not: ~~a money~~)	Only count nouns can have *a*, *an*, or a number in front of them.
I need (**some**) new winter **boots**.	I need (**some**) **luggage** for my trip.	Both count and noncount nouns can use *some*.
I have **a pair of sunglasses**. He has **ten pairs of shoes** in his closet.	**a piece of** / **two pieces of jewelry** **a cup of** / **two cups of coffee** **a glass of** / **two glasses of water**	You can use *a pair of* to count items that are always plural (*pants, glasses, pajamas, headphones*) and items that come in twos (*shoes, gloves, earrings*). You can also make some noncount nouns countable by adding words like *a piece of*, *a cup of*, *a glass of*.

Some common noncount nouns:
- Collective items: *clothing, jewelry, money, luggage, furniture*
- Certain food and drink items: *bread, rice, fruit, meat, water, coffee, tea, milk*
- Abstract ideas: *life, time, love, information, evidence*

A 🔁 Complete the dialogs with *a(n)* or nothing. Then practice with a partner.

1. A: Your dad wears _____ jewelry, right?

   B: Yes. He wears _____ wedding ring.

2. A: I need _____ new pair of gloves. Let's go shopping.

   B: I can't. I have _____ homework.

3. A: Can I have _____ money for the bus?

   B: Sure. Here's _____ dollar.

4. A: I need _____ information about fashion design classes.

   B: There's _____ link on the school website. Check it out.

5. A: I'm bringing _____ luggage on the plane. Are you?

   B: Yeah, I have _____ small bag.

B 🔁 Imagine you are going to Lima for a week. Make a list of clothes and other items you need. Finish the sentences with count or noncount nouns. Then compare your ideas with a partner.

1. I need some _____ for my trip.

2. I also have to get _____ and some _____.

3. And finally, I need a(n) _____, two _____, and a pair of _____.

I have to get some snacks for the plane.

Questions and Answers with *How much* / *How many*	
Count nouns	**Noncount nouns**
How many parks are there in your city?	**How much** pollution is there?

	Count nouns	Noncount nouns

Affirmative	(There are) **a lot / many.**
	          some / a few.
	          two.
		(There's) **a lot.**
		          some / a little.
		          ---------- 	

Negative	There are**n't many.** / **Not many.** There are**n't any.** / **None.**	There is**n't much.** / **Not much.** There is**n't any.** / **None.**

How many is used with count nouns. *How much* is used with noncount nouns.

A few means a very small number of something.

It's common to answer *How much* / *How many* questions with a short answer:

(*There are*) *a lot* (*of parks*).   (*There's*) *a little* (*pollution*).

The short answers in the negative are *Not many, Not much,* and *None.*

A Circle the best word to complete each sentence.

1. There isn't many / any traffic on the road at the moment.

2. Yesterday, there was a lot of smog, but today, there's only a little / a few.

3. How many / much people live in your neighborhood?

4. A: How many / much rain does this city get in the winter?

    B: It gets a lot / much.

B Complete the dialogs with the words in **bold** in the chart.

1. A: How _____ bookstores are there in this city?

    B: Not _____. Most people buy books online now.

2. A: How _____ traffic is there at 8:30 in the morning?

    B: There's _____. You can be stuck in traffic for an hour or more.

3. A: How _____ friends do you have?

    B: _____. I just moved here. I only know one or two people.

4. A: How _____ homework do we have tonight?

    B: _____. The teacher didn't give us any.

5. A: Do you have _____ free time on the weekend?

    B: I have _____, about an hour or two.

6. A: How _____ Thai restaurants are there in your city?

    B: There are _____. We don't even have one Thai restaurant.

C 🔁 Now ask and answer the questions in **B** with a partner. Use your own answers.

Answers

Answers to page 15, Communication: Personality Quiz, Exercise B

Green	Blue	Purple	Orange
You're generous and you care about other people. You want to help them. But sometimes, you're too picky! Remember, people aren't perfect.	You're ambitious and a little bit reserved. But remember—it's important to smile. Don't be so serious all the time!	You love to learn and try new things. You're also very bright. But sometimes, you're too competitive. Let others win once in a while!	You're interesting, and you love adventure. But be careful! Sometimes you're very impulsive! Remember to think about your future, too!

NOTES

NOTES

NOTES

NOTES

NOTES

NOTES

NOTES